PRAISE FOR
A JOURNEY THROUGH TIME AND CULTURE:
MEMOIR OF A PSYCHIATRIST

"Based upon serious reflection and candid articulation, *A Journey Through Time and Culture* is not only a remarkable legacy of Dr. Ramesh Shah to his family and friends, but can also be a great source of courage and inspiration to countless others who only dream but never get started to tell their life story."

— Baldev K. Seekri
Author of *Organizational Turnarounds*, *Seizing Success*, and *Meaningful Aging* and Former General Manager of Texas Instruments Inc.

"What an AMAZING journey and tremendous story! I applaud you for publishing your private moments so others can learn and benefit. Kudos for a job well done, my friend. I'm inspired!!!"

— T.J. Valente M.D.
Associate Professor, *Department of Psychiatry*, University of South Florida, College of Medicine, Tampa
Assistant Professor, University of Central Florida Medical School, Orlando
Director of Lifestream Behavioral Center
Leesburg, Florida

A JOURNEY THROUGH
TIME AND CULTURE

with best wishes,

Ramen

A JOURNEY THROUGH TIME AND CULTURE

MEMOIR OF A PSYCHIATRIST

RAMESH C. SHAH, MD

To order additional copies of this book, contact:
Xlibris
1-888-795-4274
www.Xlibris.com
Orders@Xlibris.com
802861

DEDICATION

This book is dedicated to my wife, Meenakshi, to my daughters, Shefali and Shilpi (Paulomi), to my son-in-laws, Pranav and Arpan, and my dear grandchildren, Raya, Ayana, Sahana, and Saavan.

CONTENTS

ACKNOWLEDGEMENTS

I would like to extend my deep appreciation to Mr. Baldev Seekri for his continued guidance and encouragement in writing this memoir. I am grateful to my brother, Mukesh, and also to Dr. Chandra Mehrotra, Dr. Mohan Nadar, Ms. Sandhya Mankodi, Ms. Reshma Parekh, Dr. Atul Shah, Dr. Jairam Rajan and Dr. Thomas Valente who provided invaluable suggestions after reading my manuscript.

To Ms. Mary Ann Revell, a writing teacher and adjunct instructor of English, for her writing recommendations during my classes at Lake Sumpter State College in Leesburg, Florida. To Linda Hurley, for her initial editing on my manuscript and to the staff of Xlibris (Ms. Louise Panelo and Ms. Kaye Parsons, especially) for final editing, printing, and publication of this book.

To my wife and best friend Meena, who has walked beside me through life's endeavors, challenges, and adventures. I would like to extend my profound gratitude for the patience, love, and sacrifice she has shown in our marriage and journey together.

To my daughter Shefali, for whom I am thankful for her unconditional love, for her help and guidance in writing my manuscript, and for the cherished advice she has given me in different aspects of life. The pride I feel as a father to see her follow in my footsteps in efforts to improve mental health as a service to her community is beyond words.

To my daughter Shilpi, who walks with a determined spirit and a soft heart. I am thankful for her love and support. She has motivated me to try to be an example of empathy, strength, and humility as a parent.

To my nephew Kuntal Vora, for the technical expertise and support he has offered me during the writing process.

To my parents, who introduced me to the discovery of new worlds through travel, and taught me the importance of family and the value of education and literature. To my siblings Anupama, Shobhana, Mukesh, and all my dear friends for their love and support throughout the years. I have been blessed to have you in my life.

To the teachers I have had throughout my educational career and the attending psychiatrists who mentored me in our field, becoming your colleague as a psychiatrist is one of my great accomplishments.

To the mental health staff that worked alongside me throughout my professional career, I enjoyed our journey together in treating countless patients. Most importantly, I want to thank all my patients for allowing and trusting me to treat them and for enriching my life in return. I hope that I have been able to help them as much as they have helped me.

To the readers, thanks for choosing to learn about my life in this memoir. I hope I have shed some light on unique experiences that I may have had and that you find a sense of camaraderie in parallel experiences in your own lives.

Finally, I would like to thank God for giving me strength and guidance during the good and bad times.

Gratefully yours,
Ramesh Shah

CHAPTER 1

THE SCHOOL YEARS

At Lawrence School - Lovedale, India

I was sent away to the Lawrence School in 1955 at the age of eleven. The private paramilitary school was located in the small town of Lovedale in the Nilgiris mountains, seven thousand feet above sea level. It was approximately a five-hour drive from my hometown of Calicut (Kozhikode), which is found in the tropical state of Kerala in South India.

Sir Henry Lawrence, the founder, was trained in a military academy in England and then joined the British Bengal Artillery in India. In 1845, he proposed to the Indian government that they establish asylums in parts of India. One was set up in Sanawar, near Punjab in the north in 1846; the other in the Nilgiris mountains in 1858. These institutions were originally established for the education of the orphaned Indian children of European soldiers. His purpose was to develop well-rounded citizens grounded in Christian values that would be both physically and emotionally strong. Sir Henry Lawrence continues to be commemorated on the 14th of May each year on Founder's Day; marked by a parade, speeches by dignitaries, and other ceremonies.

The school curriculum gradually evolved over the years to include British military traditions which are still prevalent today. In 1949, after India received independence from the British, the school was handed over to the Indians. The name was changed from Lawrence Memorial Royal Military School to, simply, Lawrence School. On that day, the governor reminded the school to uphold the traditions of the past and give allegiance to the new Indian tricolor flag and country. He also told Lawrencians to continue to strive toward high achievements in education, discipline and sports.

On my first day of school, my parents and I were taken on a tour. The school resembled a British castle, made of rocks and bricks with a big clock tower in the center. The main building had four boys' dormitories with attached quarters for the housemasters and were named for mountain ranges: Aravalli, Nilgiris, Vindhya and Sumeru. The house masters, staff and students hailed from all parts of the country; thus, the school represented a mini-India. A large hall served as a venue for meetings, school functions, plays, movie shows, and ballroom dancing. The dining hall could serve nearly two hundred at one seating. Not far away, but out of sight, was the girls' hostel housing approximately one hundred students in two dormitories. The girls came to the main building for classes and other functions. There was also a prep school for young kids aged up to 8 years. The school had three large playgrounds, an outdoor swimming pool, and a stable for the horses. The students came from well-to-do families who could afford to pay the expensive tuition fees. The school also had a sizable number of Anglo-Indians, where one of the parents was British and the other was Indian.

It was difficult for me to get adjusted to this strange military-type school culture. Pangs of separation anxiety from my parents and a feeling of sadness swept over me, even though my two cousins were there. It took a few weeks for me to settle in.

We wore different uniforms for sports and outdoor activities, for classes, for military parade training, plus dress blues for special functions, such as the Founder's Day parade and formal dinners. Each dormitory had about sixty beds and a locker for each student. We were responsible for keeping our areas clean and tidy. We were punished if we did not keep our locker clean.

The school had head boys and head girls and each house had a prefect. Some of the prefects were chosen by the housemaster based on their physical strength so that they could keep control over the rest of the boys. This was understandable to some extent because some boys were hard to control.

Some of the students seemed to have psychological problems, such as severe attention deficit hyperactivity or conduct disorder, and were difficult to get along with. My weak physical constitution caused me to be pushed around during my initial years, though I tried to put up a fight many times. I was punched in the face once, causing my lip to be cut and require stitches. While this caused some resentment on my part, I continued my attempt to adjust to the tough environment. Some housemasters kept themselves aloof and did not interfere much in our daily life. I thought that it might all be part of upholding the school's intention to make us strong and resilient; part of our "character building."

The school certainly had its share of caring teachers, housemasters and prefects, as well as many kids with good moral character and manners. I befriended those kids and we enjoyed many happy times together. It was with such a group that I spent my five years at Lawrence. In the end, perhaps the school environment gave me the character to never give in and to overcome obstacles. It also made me a well-rounded person.

Our daily routine was tightly regimented. We woke to the sound of the bugle at 6am, followed by a chotta snack in the dining room (a sweet bun and a cup of tea). After that we had to run the mountainous roads in our shorts, regardless of the weather conditions. Then we had the military "trooping of the color" (parade with rifles). The morning culminated with breakfast, followed by a school assembly during which a teacher gave a short speech and we sang religious hymns. One such hymn was written by the famous Indian poet Rabindranath Tagore. Then we had various classes until 1pm, lunch, and then games and sports from 2 until 4pm.

Our strenuous activities done for the day, we formed a line for the few shower bathrooms. The older and bigger boys always pushed their weight around and passed by us to get in first. It routinely took hours before I could get my turn. Being of a sensitive nature, the unfairness of all this was overwhelming at times, but all I could do was carry on. The shower was followed by dinner, then prep studies on our own until we went to bed at 9pm.

Though we probably spent more time in physical and extracurricular activities than in studies; we were expected to maintain high grades. This type of daily routine instilled discipline in my life and gave me my first taste of what British military tradition was like. The school food was not the best, but it was enough to fuel our growth spurts and energy. I missed my mother's delicious home cooking. I, along with my cousins, chose to be vegetarians based on our Jain beliefs of non-violence. This certainly did not help to build up my muscles to compete with the bigger and more muscular boys.

For special dinners, known as "bada khana," all the boys would gather in the big mess hall. The school prefect would start with a prayer; "For what we are about to receive may the Lord make us truly thankful." The school had a huge kitchen with several cooks and servants. It was located a short distance from the mess hall, so the food would come in huge trolley cars on railway tracks. We had to dress up in school uniform and eat British style, with knives and forks. The menu would consist of chicken biryani for non-vegetarians and vegetarian biryani for vegetarians. Biryani is an Indian rice dish made with plenty of spices. This is often accompanied by a spicy chicken curry and a delicious trifle pudding. We always looked forward to this great feast.

There was no doubt that this was a unique school, often compared to prestigious Eton, in England. We were groomed to become well-rounded persons by taking part in activities not available in other Indian schools. Lawrence was affiliated with England's University of Cambridge and the prestigious diploma we received was known as "Senior Cambridge" as opposed to the matriculation diploma students received from other schools.

We had three main sport seasons: cricket in spring, soccer in summer (during the monsoon season), and field hockey in fall. It was enjoyable playing these games in sport fields like top flats, middle flats and grass pitch. However, once the inter-house competitions started, the spirit of sportsmanship disappeared. If our team lost, we would be punished.

We organized "Ked fight" between two houses, so named for the Keds sneaker brand. We would collect our shoes and then proceed to throw them, like missiles, at the members of the opposite house. It was great fun as long as you did not get hurt!

There were also track and field events, gymnastics, and boxing. During one such competition, a boy accidentally threw a 25-pound shot put on my toe. I was carried to the school hospital, run by an ex-army physician, where I was kept for a few days until I recovered. It was hard to be in the hospital without nurturing parents being around; I missed them.

But I was feisty and did not give in easily. Once a bigger boy was harassing me. I challenged him to a "com", what we used to call a fight. We wrestled and punched at each other until I had to give up since I could no longer fight. After that fight, the bigger boy never harassed me.

While I took part in these athletic and sports events, I did not excel. Boys with weak physiques, like mine, were looked down upon and called "slops." Unable to excel in sports and with average grades, I feel I developed a low self-esteem and mild anxiety. This continued to plague me, somewhat, throughout my life. However, I was proud of being able to stand up for myself.

But there were happy moments, too. I did enjoy horseback riding. The school had five horses in various sizes, from small to large. Our riding master taught us English riding. We were taught to post on stirrups when the horse was trotting on its four legs. We would sit on the saddle when the horse would canter on its two legs and we would stand on the stirrups when the horse would have its four legs in the air when galloping. On one such ride, my mount, a big horse, took off, galloping away from the rest of the group with me on its back. I prayed that I would not fall and hurt myself or get killed. Finally, after a long distance, the horse tired and stopped on its own. Luckily, I was not hurt and over the years, with practice, I enjoyed galloping on the mountains.

One of the more grueling events of the year was the cross-country foot race. The five-mile race began at the main building and passed over forest paths in the hills surrounding the school. We had to run through some pretty rough terrain including wet bogs. I remember having a "stitch" (a severe pain) in the right side of my abdomen, halfway through the course. The cheerleaders stationed along the way made sure that we kept on the path and kept running, despite being tired. We were glad to reach the grass pitch at the bottom of the mountain. During the last stretch we had to jump off the first waterfall, which was about seven to eight feet in height. After coming out of the waterfall, we ran a short distance to a second waterfall and landed in a pool filled with waist high cold mountain water. There were a couple of lifeguards stationed in the pool, in case somebody fainted! Once I came out of the pool, I laid down, exhausted and out of breath, and could hardly hear the girls cheering our team. An ambulance was also stationed at the finish line for medical emergencies. The first three runners to finish got the trophies, but I was just glad to finish the race safe and sound. I also took part in the annual 'boot march', nearly thirteen miles in the hot sun, on mountainous roads.

One of the more enjoyable activities was the camping experience in the mountains, dubbed pleasure camp. Though challenging, it was exciting and fun to be on our own and to rely on one another to survive. Six boys would be given a tent, food, water and other supplies which would barely last a week. We were left on our own near a river in the forest to survive and live on our own for a week. Our teacher said "I don't care whether you beg, borrow or steal food. But you have to survive on your own if your food runs out." We set up our own tents, started a fire and tried to cook our own food. The food turned out to be edible most of the time. At night we would bundle up near the fire so that we would not freeze and played games with other campers.

The annual NCC (National Cadet Corps) camp consisted of groups of boys from different public schools in India. The following schools usually took part: Lawrence, Sanawar; Rajkumar College, Rajkot, Gujarat; Scindia School, Gwalior MP; Mayo College, Ajmer, Rajasthan; and Doons School in Dehradun UP. Many of these schools also had military traditions. Some were started and run by the royal families of their respective states. Besides military drills we also competed in a lot of games. Once the camp was held near the military academy, in the old army barracks near Khadakwasla, Pune. The barracks stood in a huge field, covered with tin semicircular roofs, and surrounded by snake pits. We were told to carry our field hockey sticks wherever we went so that we could try to kill any snake we saw! Needless to say, we had trouble sleeping at night!

Learning to shoot was a requirement. We would lie on our belly in the indoor shooting range and point our .22 rifles at targets about thirty yards away. Our instructor, Abe, was quite well known for his courage. Our Nilgiris hills were near Mudumalai and Bandipur forests where wild elephants and a few tigers abounded. When he heard that a tiger had wandered to a hill near the school, he was sent there in a lorry to shoot it. He, along with another brave man, did shoot the tiger and brought it back. I was fortunate enough to see it. This incident reminded me of the book "Man Eaters of Kumaon," about Jim Corbett, a legendary 19th century British hunter. He was sent to shoot man-eating tigers that were terrorizing the local village people, in the jungles of Kumaon hills in northern India. He chased these clever tigers, all alone, for many months until he was able to track them down and shoot them. There is a national park named after him in north India.

When I was seventeen, my uncle's family from Kerala and another family from Chennai decided to see wild elephants in Mudumalai. My two cousins and I joined them. We stayed in a dak bungalow inside the jungle. We could hear noises of wild buffaloes, elephants, and other animals at night. With no electric lights, it was pitch dark. Despite being somewhat frightened, I was able to get some sleep. We awakened early in the morning to the sound of the many different types of birds. At sunrise, fifteen of us mounted five elephants, fitted with seats on their backs so that we could sit comfortably. The mahout (elephant driver) sat on top of the elephant's head and steered it with a stick. These elephants had been trained to take travelers deep inside the jungle walking in a caravan; the mahouts taking their directions from the position of the sun. After traveling for two hours without spotting any wild animals, as bad luck would have it, the lead elephant accidentally hit a beehive in a bush. Thousands of bees swarmed and started stinging the elephants and us. The frightened elephants started running to get away from the bees and the mahouts could not control them. The silence of the jungle was shattered by our screams. We were trying to hold on to our seats and at the same time ward off the bees. In the confusion, my aunt's shawl fell to the ground. To our surprise, her elephant stopped, picked up the shawl with its trunk and gave it back to her, before starting to run again. To our relief, the bees disappeared after about ten minutes and the elephants stopped running. This was certainly a scary moment for all of us.

After being fortunate enough to spot a herd of wild elephants with babies, we returned to our bungalow safely. The bee stings made our skin itchy and painful. We were far from the nearest town with a clinic and had only Nilgiri oil, extracted from eucalyptus trees, to rub on our bodies. It hardly helped. That same night, one of our fellow travelers had a severe chest pain, probably due to anxiety. Again, the only thing we could do was to rub the Nilgiris oil on his chest! He was alright the next day. We had all survived and came out of the jungle safe and sound.

One of my father's friends, Ashok, made a similar jungle trip to Mudumalai forest a few months later. He was not so lucky. Once a year a young bull elephant becomes manic and somewhat aggressive due to increased testosterone being secreted. The rest of the herd kicks this 'mad elephant' out of the herd, due to his erratic behavior, and he roams around the jungle alone looking for a suitable female. While Ashok was riding along with a mahout, looking for a wild elephant herd, they encountered one such rogue elephant. It started attacking the tame male elephant head on. The mahout took his small spear, and superficially pierced the rogue elephant's eye. That temporarily stopped the attack, allowing them to get away. Ashok lived to tell his story.

Elephants were often the scourge of truckers and other motorists. To reach Mudumalai Forest, from the plains of Kerala, truckers took a mountainous road known as Anna Ghat, or Elephant Mountain. While such encounters are rare, an elephant could push the truck down into the valley. Fearing that these wild elephants may attack them, the truck drivers take out their shirts, soak them in petrol from their gas tank, and set the shirts on fire, scaring the elephants away!

We had one such encounter, during the daytime, on our recent visit to India. A wild elephant was grazing and blocking our road near the Bandipur Forest. Our driver decided to wait at a safe distance, hoping the elephant would cross the road to the other side. The elephant took its own sweet time and after about 45 minutes decided to cross the road, whereupon, the driver put on the gas and sped away, to our relief! Enough of elephant stories!

Dignitaries would visit our school from time to time, like India's Foreign Minister, Mr. Krishna Menon. We were also lucky to have India's Prime Minister Nehru, his daughter Indira Gandhi, and the Chief Minister of Tamil Nadu, Kamaraj Nadar. I heard Nehru's ex tempore speech, given in the large hall. He said he had heard great things about the school and was happy to meet young boys and girls studying, to shoulder the burden of India when they grew up. He noted that we were fortunate to receive training, not only in studies, but in personal character building. He spoke on the diversity of our country, made up of millions of people speaking different languages and practicing different faiths. He highlighted the disparity between the rich and the vast number of poor. He wanted to uplift these people. He went on to say that India was united despite these differences. He called on us to do big things once we grew up and to serve our country since we were the citizens of tomorrow.

In 1959, after spending five years at Lawrence School, I was ready to go on to college. Being an average student, I received my diploma in division three rather than division one. I hoped to do better in college. But I had survived the harsh school environment and learned to face difficulties with resilience, discipline, and courage. This positive attitude was to help me overcome many obstacles and setbacks, which I encountered later in my life. It provided the opportunity to associate with boys from different ethnic backgrounds, instilling a feeling of tolerance. In addition, I acquired better command of English and Hindi languages, which would eventually serve me well. My task going forward was overcoming the anxiety that had developed during my tenure at Lawrence. But, I would try to live up the school motto, "never give in." Little did I know that my life was to change in different ways after I left the Lawrence School.

Recently, on a visit to India, I learned that the school still enjoys an excellent reputation and there is a waiting list for admission. It has produced some high achieving alumni over the years, to include Indian military officers. The school continues to boast a well-educated faculty who impart a high quality, well-rounded education to its seven hundred students. In hindsight, my experiences at this school taught me about my personal strength and weaknesses. It had a strong influence on pursuing my career of choice and how I would approach my relationships with family and patients.

Lawrence School, Lovedale

CHAPTER 2

MUMBAI, INDIA

Following my graduation from Lawrence, at the age of 17, my father sent me to Mumbai (Bombay) for my college education. I assume he felt that the colleges in Calicut were not of a high standard and that Mumbai would provide better career opportunities. Thousands of Indians flock there for education, jobs and the opportunity to start a business. The colleges offer education in science, commerce, arts, engineering and the law. Though I had visited Mumbai many times, it took some time for me to get used to a densely populated metropolitan city. It was a big transition from an isolated high school in the lush Nilgiris mountains.

Mumbai is the financial capital of India, the equivalent of New York City. The population is multicultural, with several ethnic and religious communities contributing to its growth and vibrancy. A sizable number of its population belongs to my Gujarati community, renowned for their business skills and wealth. Several of my relatives reside there. Though I had observed my father at work, I had no business skills. I was expected to get my degree and make a living on my own. I was grateful to him for financing my education.

My father's Kerala-based umbrella company had a branch office and a store on Princess Street in Mumbai. Occasionally, he would visit this office and meet with his brother and three sisters, and their families. We would take these opportunities to spend some time together.

Having received no formal guidance regarding what school to attend, what courses to take, or what career to pursue, I may have been influenced by my uncle and aunt who were physicians. They had graduated from a Mumbai medical school and had a successful practice in Dhulia. My mother had also encouraged me to be a doctor. I could have pursued a career in engineering, landing a good job in one of the new industries coming up in India. However, I was poor in math and had no interest in engineering. Although my father was in business, he did not encourage me along those lines, and I was not drawn to it. There was not much money to be made in the field of liberal arts and because Biology was more of my strength, my interest inclined toward the medical profession. I chose to apply to multiple science colleges and traveled long distances on a bus, in a crowded city with heavy traffic, to get to my college admission interviews. I gained admission to a National college in Bandra, a suburb of Mumbai.

I immersed myself in my curriculum, foregoing parties and extracurricular activities, and received high grades on my first-year science final examination. After many years of mediocre performance at Lawrence School, this made me very happy. My emphasis for the next few years would be to dedicate myself to my studies. This determination was strengthened by the Ramakrishna Mission hostel where I boarded. In their early morning lectures and prayers, the Swamis taught us to lead a life of self-control, austerity, purity, contentment, detachment, peace, humility and tolerance. I made a few friends there and was much happier in this spiritual place than I had in the military atmosphere of Lawrence.

In my sophomore year, I obtained admission to Jai Hind College, in affluent south Mumbai; a prestigious interscience school with an emphasis on biology. My life was about to change once again because these students were brighter and more intelligent than those in National College, the cream of the crop of Bombay schools. The atmosphere was highly competitive, and they were scoring higher grades than I was in chemistry, physics, biology, English and Hindi. However, I tried my best to keep up my grades.

As part of the biology course curriculum, we had to dissect an earthworm and a lobster to expose their nervous systems. These procedures seemed somewhat cruel to me. My performance anxiety during the interscience final examinations most likely affected my results. I missed admission to a Mumbai medical college by just a few points. My participation in the NCC (National Cadet Corp), a paramilitary organization with weekend drills, earned me bonus grades at the end of the year which might have boosted my final grades to allow admission. However, I had misplaced my certificate and when I approached my sergeant to issue a replacement, he rebuked me for my carelessness and refused. So, my destiny was to change once again. Sadly, I had to say goodbye to Mumbai, a vibrant city I had started to like, and find an alternative medical school.

CHAPTER 3

KASTURBA MEDICAL COLLEGE MANIPAL, INDIA

Ramesh (second from right)
with friends at KMC, Manipal

Kasturba Medical College (KMC), was in the lush green countryside town of Manipal in the coastal Karnataka state. Nothing was happening in this small town until Dr. T.M.A. Pai conceived the notion to start India's first private medical college. In 1962, the college campus consisted of a couple of main buildings, a library, a hospital, a boys' hostel, a girls' hostel and a soccer field. The medical faculty lived in small houses surrounding the campus.

Until then, India had government-run public medical schools in each state and the tuition fees were subsidized. This allowed bright students who could not afford the full tuition to attend. KMC required a small monetary donation and therefore, attracted students from well-to-do families. By this time, I was becoming more interested in the human body and the diseases that could affect it. Encouraged by my father to apply, I did well on my entrance exam and interview.

The Bachelor of Medicine and Bachelor of Surgery degree (MBBS) was a four-and-a-half-year course. The initial one-and-a-half-years took place in Manipal, with the rest completed in Mangalore. KMC also attracted a few American students who were not able to get admission to their own medical schools. They generally kept to themselves, though they seemed to be a friendly bunch. They roamed about wearing ponchos to keep from getting wet in the monsoon rains. They hoped to do well enough in the first year-and-a-half to transfer to an American medical school. An African American professor, through an affiliation with an American university, visited our school and gave excellent lectures in anatomy, though we had some difficulty in understanding his accent.

I became keenly interested in studying first year subjects such as anatomy, physiology, and biochemistry. Reading "Grey's Anatomy" fascinated me with its beautiful illustrations and descriptions of body parts. I was also keenly interested in physiology, the functions of different body parts. Biochemistry was a little difficult to understand. I was struck by the thought that there must be a great creator out there to have made such a wonderful and near perfect body. I was impressed by some of our teachers who were both highly knowledgeable about their subjects and quite articulate in their lectures. Although our classroom consisted of more than a hundred students, the lecturer took control of the class and gave lectures without microphones, using blackboards for illustrations, unlike the high-tech computer based methods employed today. The girls occupied the first three benches and the boys the rest. Some boys were more interested in looking at the girls than listening to the lecturer.

We had some amusing moments in the anatomy room. We were required to dissect human cadavers so that we could identify and study different parts of the body. A cadaver was shared by four male medical students, each wearing white aprons with deep pockets, each extremity dissected by a different student. During the dissection of one upper extremity, I was away for a month on mandatory NCC training. By the time I returned, the whole upper extremity had been dissected, weakening my knowledge of the anatomy of that part of the body!

Our anatomy dissection room had a strange pet, a huge python in a cage. To feed it, a servant would place a small, live rabbit in the cage through a one-way opening. Upon seeing the python, the rabbit would freeze, as if hypnotized. Slowly the python would put the rabbit in its mouth and swallow it whole. Thank goodness it was placed in the corner of the room away from us, so we could avoid watching this gruesome spectacle. We did not understand why this python was placed in the anatomy dissection room; it had nothing to do with human anatomy. I presumed that somebody may have also been interested in reptile zoology!

Our medical school's dean was elderly and quite a strict disciplinarian. The boys' hostel was located on one side of the main medical school building and the ladies' hostel was located on the other, surrounded by a wall for security. The boys were forbidden to visit or enter the girls' hostel building; however, this did not prevent some from climbing over the wall at night and meeting their girlfriends. The dean knew that the rules were being broken, so he instructed a few brave boys, including me, to hold flashlights and hide in the bushes that surrounded the wall. The dean himself hid in the bushes with us, armed with a whistle. In the middle of the night, boys began to climb the wall. The dean blew his whistle and we ran and apprehended them. They were appropriately disciplined and from then on, the medical students knew that the dean meant business. The behavior on campus improved substantially after that.

Between attending classes and reading medical textbooks late into the night, we hardly had time for any other activities. The first year MBBS finals consisted of a handwritten examination. The practical side of the anatomy examination consisted of naming correct body parts on a cadaver or a skeleton. We were also given slides to examine under a microscope and told to identify different types of white blood cells and parasites. The examiners would then go through our answers and determine what sort of grades we made. All this was grueling, and my performance anxiety made it more difficult to pass this exam. I particularly dreaded the interviews conducted by outside examiners who asked some really tough questions.

Ramesh (far left) at National Cadet Corps Camp

CHAPTER 4

KASTURBA MEDICAL COLLEGE MANGALORE, INDIA

Medical School Days

When I received my examination results, I was delighted and relieved that I had earned a passing grade in both anatomy and physiology! Now I was ready to move to the coastal city of Mangalore to pursue the rest of my medical education. This was my fourth move in ten years, to four different states each with a language, culture and dietary habits of its own. I had been away from home since the age of eleven, living in dormitories and hostels. Although I felt like a gypsy, life was certainly exciting with different experiences, people and environments. It was certainly a lesson in adjustment.

Mangalore was a medium sized port city on the Arabian Sea in 1965 and the harbor was still under construction. Now, it hosts international cruises that start from Mumbai in the north, touching the ports of Goa, Mangalore and Cochin before heading further south towards the Indian Ocean and Colombo, Sri Lanka. Many tourists enjoy these tropical cities, with their beaches lined with coconut trees. Mangalore has several cultures and four languages are spoken there. Though the majority are Hindus, there is a sizable Christian and Muslim population. Tourist attractions include the 9th century Mangaladevi Temple and 17th century Milagres Roman Catholic Church, built by Portuguese Bishop de Castro. It was subsequently destroyed, and a new church was built in 1811. Portuguese explorer, Vasco Da Gama, landed near there in 1498, thus paving the way for the French, and ultimately the British. Since I left in 1968, it has grown by leaps and bounds, now home to industries, such as, information technology, petroleum, chemical, and shipbuilding. Mangalore port handles 75 percent of India's coffee and cashew exports.

When I arrived, in 1965, the campus consisted of a main building with many classrooms and a large auditorium which, in addition to being utilized for classes and lectures by eminent visiting professors, served as a performing arts center hosting plays and various entertainment programs, including singing of popular Indian movie songs. The highlight of the year was when our teachers produced and acted in their own play. Since KMC did not have a hospital of its own, the medical students used the Government Wenlock and Lady Goschen Hospitals for clinical rounds, with some limited association with the nearby tuberculosis sanitarium.

Our curriculum for the second MBBS consisted of pathology, bacteriology, pharmacology, forensic medicine, and toxicology. Pathology, the study of the causes and effects of diseases, included anatomic pathology (gross examination of body parts) and clinical pathology (diagnosis of diseases through the analysis of fluids and tissues). "Boyd's Pathology" was well illustrated with photographs and drawings of diseased organs. It was amazing to see a healthy organ, such as the lung, being transformed into an ugly colored organ of a different consistency, after contracting pneumonia. This was true for most of the other organs of the body, especially when they were ravaged by cancerous growths. This knowledge cautioned me to take good care of my body to avoid disease.

Our professors and teachers were highly knowledgeable and dedicated to teaching their assigned medical students, the majority of which were hardworking and eager to acquire new knowledge. However, there were occasions when it would take a few minutes for a lecturer to control the class and resume teaching. One of our instructors was a big man who did not put up with any misbehavior. Once, when he was about to start teaching a large class, some tough and rowdy students disrupted the class by making loud noises. The instructor shouted at the disruptive students, saying "Shut up", whereupon the whole class hushed so that you could have heard a pin drop. The misbehaving students knew that he was going to physically tackle them if they did not start behaving.

The forensic medicine class was interesting. It is a branch of medicine dealing with the application of medical knowledge to establish facts in legal cases, such as, suspicious deaths. Our professor had authored a book complete with gory illustrations and photographs of people who were murdered by various means. He had been instrumental in solving some difficult cases.

This reminds me of an incident that occurred in 1963. Anatomy class required each student to purchase human skeletal bones for study purposes. I had found such bones in a mail order catalog store and when they arrived at my home, they were coated with a light transparent color for preservation purposes. I piled the bones neatly in a cardboard box, and then traveled by bus to KMC Manipal. Upon boarding, the bus driver questioned me about the contents of the box. When I explained that I was taking human skeleton bones to medical college for anatomy studies, he did not believe me. To rule out foul play, he held up the bus and called the local police, who arrived in short order. After questioning me thoroughly, the officer was convinced that I had not committed any crime. Luckily, I did not have to call my forensic medicine professor to get me out of the predicament!

I was particularly interested in pharmacology, the study of drug action which influences a cell or organ of a human body. I was fascinated by how these drugs worked to cure diseases. I learned that one of the earliest pharmacologists, Charak, was born in India in 300 BC. He was one of the early contributors to Ayurveda, the traditional Hindu system of medicine, which is based on the idea of balance in bodily systems. He authored the medical treatise known as "Charak Samhita." which emphasizes healthy lifestyle, diet, oil massages, herbal medicines, yoga exercises, and meditation to prevent and cure illnesses. Ayurveda is gaining popularity in India and the west, along with other alternative systems of medicine. However, at KMC we were taught the conventional or allopathy school of medicine, with emphasis on using drugs to counter symptoms. Lacking modern medications in the 60s, we were taught about the use of liquid mixtures, tablets and antibiotics (penicillin, streptomycin and sulfadiazine) to cure common diseases.

I had to really concentrate on my lectures and then spend hours in the college library pouring over medical books to keep up my grades. In April of 1965, I was rewarded for my hard work. I was promoted to the third MBBS semester and was ready to face the challenges of my final months in medical college.

Getting used to my new hostel life in Mangalore was another matter. This three-story building was located a few miles away in the suburb known as Kaprigudda. Four of us shared a small room with a common bathroom. Additional restrooms were shared by the wing. In such tight quarters, we learned to adjust to each other's studying and sleeping habits in an effort not to disturb our roommates. Mediocre hostel food did not help to relieve stress. Sometimes the rice that was served had small stones in it. But we managed and looked forward to the day when we could afford better food. Though we competed with each other for the best grades, I was lucky to have good roommates who generally got along well with each other. We still keep in touch and get together to reminisce about the good old days when I am visiting India.

Since there was no bus service, the distance from campus necessitated private transportation. The students from well-to-do families were able to afford motorcycles or mopeds, which we called scooters. They would compete to see who could buy the fanciest, biggest, noisiest bike. My father was not easily convinced to buy me a moped; he was most likely concerned about my safety. I found navigating Mangalore traffic on a scooter to be an adventure and the avoidance of the massive and numerous potholes to be an art. The potholes were the result of heavy monsoon rains from May to September, and the inability of the city to keep up with the repairs. I always had a buddy on the back of my scooter and when I failed to successfully maneuver around a deep pothole, I would lose control, causing myself and my passenger to hit the ground. Every time we fell, my buddy would cuss me, which hurt me more than the bruises I sustained!

We had our share of students who came from rich families and, forced to attend by their parents, were not serious about their studies. Some of them partied often; sporadically getting into physical altercations with rival factions in the hostel. My friends and I tried to keep a low profile and concentrate on our studies.

Though my friends and I had consumed alcohol in moderation, we had never gotten drunk. Being curious, we decided to buy some Indian whiskey, since we could not afford imported Scotch whiskey. After drinking a couple of ounces, and not receiving the desired effect, we decided to go to the street and buy some cheap country liquor. We did not realize that it could be adulterated with unknown toxic substances. I took only a couple of ounces before my legs felt weak and buckled under me. I fell to the floor and started to throw up. I could not move my arms or legs and my heart was beating fast. Rather than feeling high, I was frightened that I might die of alcohol poisoning. I pleaded to my less affected friends to take me to the hospital emergency room, but they refused, concerned that our professors and hostel warden would find out about our drunken misadventure and punish us. I had to sweat it out the whole night and then gradually recovered the next morning, by the grace of God. I did not touch alcohol after that for many years! Sometimes you learn the hard way!

A fancy new hotel had just been built in Mangalore and, as a promotion, the owner held a cabaret dance show followed by a party. My friends and I had never seen a cabaret and though we could barely afford it, we decided to go. After the cabaret, we sat on the sidelines and observed couples dancing. A few American sailors, whom we called "shippies," joined two young Indian women on the dance floor and were fighting over them. To our surprise, we recognized the women from the outpatient clinic where they had come to be treated for a sexually transmitted disease, probably syphilis. Ethically, we could not warn the sailors and even if we could, they were too drunk to listen to us.

The curriculum for my final two MBBS years consisted of general medicine, surgery, obstetrics, gynecology, lectures and hospital rounds at Government Wenlock General Hospital. Government grants allowed the hospital to treat patients who were of a lower socioeconomic class. It was a large hospital with patients overflowing in its wards, sometimes sleeping on the floor. In the outpatient department, it was typical for there to be long lines of patients waiting to be seen. Despite having a large number of patients, the hospital staff provided good care to the patients. Being a teaching hospital, the attending physician would be surrounded by medical students or interns in white apron-like lab coats, while making his rounds. We would follow from bed to bed, talking to patients about their medical history. Since we did not have advanced diagnostic equipment, such as, CT scans or MRIs, we had to depend on physical examination. We would palpate body parts and rely on our stethoscope to make a diagnosis. Most patients could not afford even an x-ray. Lab tests usually included examination of sputum, feces and urine, with minimal blood work. We students were in awe of the advanced lab and radiological procedures being used in the US that were documented in the New England Journal of Medicine and the Journal of the American Medical Association.

During my time at this hospital in the 1960s, I observed and treated many diseases while doing my internship and clinical rounds. Sometimes, the cases were unique to the tropical areas of the Indian region. For example, many of the Wenlock patients presented with mosquitoborne illnesses, rarely seen in the US and Europe; malaria and filariasis were prevalent. Malaria is contracted from an anopheles mosquito bite which then spreads parasites into the blood cells. This results in high fever, chills, and sweating. Most symptoms subside with treatment, unless the patient contracts malignant tertian malaria or blackwater fever. This is a deadly form of malaria where the red blood cells start bursting. I had contracted malaria when I was about eight years old. My parents would rub my forehead with a rubber bottle filled with ice to bring down my high temperature. Fortunately, the use of mosquito nets, repellants, eradication of mosquitoes, and the use of BCG vaccination has helped reduce the incidence of malaria in Asia and Africa. The Center for Disease Control advises tourists traveling to these countries to take prophylactic medicines against malaria, like doxycycline. Thanks to the World Health Organization (WHO) and the Bill and Melinda Gates Foundation, malaria is gradually being eradicated.

Another mosquito-borne disease often seen in India is filariasis. It is caused by a parasitic worm that is carried by mosquitoes and biting flies. One type of filariasis blocks the lymphatic system leading to the deposition of proteins and tissues causing a swelling of the leg or genitalia. Commonly, the swelling is so great that it resembles an elephant's leg, also known as elephantiasis. We had a neighbor in Calicut who suffered from elephantiasis of both his legs. Despite this, he would walk to work every day. I took Hetrazan as a preventive measure. Treatment and prevention efforts are being used in Africa and Southeast Asia by administering appropriate medication to entire communities and through mosquito control and elimination. The Carter Foundation is helping with these efforts in Africa. New mosquito borne diseases like dengue and chikungunya are spreading in India and Africa. I used to dread getting bitten by a mosquito and always slept in a mosquito net in our hostel room.

One tragic, but medically interesting case that I witnessed was a man infected with the rabies virus. He was placed in a cell where he could be observed by the medical staff. He was exhibiting advanced symptoms, such as, violent movements, excited and somewhat psychotic behavior (fear of water) and making strange noises. He was placed in an isolation ward to protect the staff from coming in touch with the patient's body fluids. With no cure for late stage rabies, he soon became unconscious and died. Some dog bite victims seek help from faith healers first, thus delaying taking the traditional preventive rabies vaccine with, ultimately, serious consequences. About 18,000 people die from rabies every year in India where rabies are more prevalent because of the large number of stray unvaccinated dogs. My cousin was bitten, and he received the rabies vaccine in his abdominal wall for nearly two weeks and did not contract the virus. Thanks to Louis Pasteur for developing the rabies vaccine.

On one of my morning rounds, I came across a patient having an aneurysm of the thoracic aorta, the large artery in the chest carrying blood from the heart to the rest of the body. This is when the wall of the artery becomes very thin and starts bulging. It is often associated with hardening of the arteries, syphilis, and aging. I could see the patient's artery bulging through his chest wall and beating. The hospital was most likely unable to provide advanced cardiovascular surgical treatments to treat his condition. Eventually, the aneurysm burst, his blood spouted like a fountain and he died.

During one of my rounds in the outpatient department, our chief was discussing the sad case of a male child, about six years old, who had a mass protruding from his rectum. At first, I thought that he may be suffering from cancer. But our chief informed us that it was most likely caused by a sexually transmitted disease. I was angered by the fact that small children were abused by predators, a fact exacerbated by the vulnerability of poor and neglected children. These issues are being addressed in modern India.

Tuberculosis (TB) was quite prevalent. TB is a bacterial-caused infection of the lungs. Worldwide, as of 2017, the CDC indicated there were about ten million reported cases, mostly in Africa and Southeast Asia. In 2015, approximately 1.8 million people died from the disease. It is highly contagious, often spread by airdrops during coughing bouts. A TB patient can infect about ten people with whom they come in close contact. One of my relatives had contracted TB and I would see her walking to the municipal clinic, every day, to receive her Streptomycin shot. Streptomycin and other medications, such as isoniazid (INH) can be effective treatments, however they did not work for her. She lost a lot of weight, and sadly, eventually died.

We diagnosed many TB cases by listening to patients' lungs with a stethoscope, since many patients could not afford a chest x-ray. These docile patients would just pray that the medical students knew the proper technique for administering the Streptomycin injections. Rarely, some patients would curse me if I caused them pain. Some patients had to undergo partial or complete removal of a lung due to cavities caused by TB. Despite encountering a large number of TB patients, the doctors rarely caught this highly contagious disease because we had been vaccinated when young, thus providing immunity.

The large number of diseases and numerous treatments in the medical textbooks made it difficult to digest and retain all the information. I was envious of some of my classmates who seemed to have a photographic memory. I had to go home and read over the lecture notes a few times and read my textbooks repeatedly to score passing grades.

In the last year of medical college, I had not yet cleared my last and final MBBS Examination. I had to study hard, late into the night, "burning the midnight oil". Unlike examinations in the US where students took a number of tests throughout the year to arrive at a cumulative grade, in India we only had one yearly exam that counted as our final grade. Therefore, there was great pressure to perform well on it. The final examination consisted of written essays in medicine, surgery, and OB/GYN. In these, I thought I had done well. The practical examinations, in medicine and surgery, consisted of examining patients, diagnosing their illness, and determining their treatment. Many of the examiners came from a rival university, which made me more anxious.

After the grueling finals, I went home to be with my parents and took a well-deserved rest. After a few weeks, I received the results and my worst fears were realized, I had failed the surgery practicals examination. I had a passing grade in all other subjects, but this was my first exam failure and it was hard on my ego. The fact that quite a few of my classmates had passed, added to my sorrow.

After a few days of grieving, I decided to try again. I returned to my hostel only to find that most students had gone home. It was a lonely and sad experience to be nearly alone in the hostel. I decided that rereading the thick surgery textbook by Bailey and Love was the best way to prepare for my examination. After three months, I took the surgery practicals examination again and once more, I was unsuccessful. When I heard the results, I broke down emotionally. I was losing confidence, afraid that I would never pass this examination. Eventually, I regained my composure and my confidence, and with the encouragement of my parents, decided to be true to my high school's motto to "never give in."

Once again, I returned to the hostel and kept reviewing the textbook of surgery. I felt quite more knowledgeable about surgical cases and their treatments. Going back, I also had the opportunity to observe more surgical cases in the hospital, which sharpened my diagnostic skills. This time a couple of my classmates, who had also failed their surgery practicals, were also there. We encouraged each other and buoyed each other's spirits. I was more confident this time and passed with flying colors. This taught me a valuable life lesson; never become disheartened by adverse events or obstacles and continue trying, again and again, until successful.

KMC is now ranked among the ten best medical colleges of India and has expanded tremendously since 1968. It boasts an excellent education for students who hail from many different countries. Today, the medical training is provided in a state-of-the-art medical college with the clinical training being provided in well-equipped modern hospitals with highly trained and dedicated staff. The students are well trained to provide medical services to the public once they graduate. Since the sixties, many KMC alumni have migrated to different countries and are successful in their medical and academic careers.

CHAPTER 5

INTERNSHIP

At Kaprigudda Hostel in Mangalore, India

I was relieved to leave my textbooks behind and begin my internship. Little did I know that I would pick them back up in a few years! My one-year rotating internship in medicine, surgery, and its sub-branches; ophthalmology, otolaryngology, dermatology, pediatrics, orthopedics, preventive medicine, and sexually transmitted diseases would be at Wenlock Hospital in Mangalore, and obstetrics and gynecology was at Lady Goschen Hospital. For my psychiatric rotation, I had to travel to the distant city of Bangalore (now Bengaluru).

During our studies, one of our professors told us about Sushrata. Surgical techniques had been practiced in India since ancient times. In the 6th century B.C., Sushruta, the founding father of modern surgery, wrote "Sushruta Samhita" in which he describes various surgical procedures, collecting equipment, prophylaxis, modes of incision, post-surgical steps, dressing of wounds, instructions to patients after surgery and measures to relieve pain. He also wrote about cauterization, letting of blood by application of leeches, and grafting.

In addition to learning the technical aspects of surgery, one of our professors discussed the emotional side of it. He told us that anything could go wrong during a surgical procedure, and despite our best efforts, the patient could die. He advised us to be strong emotionally and not let severe illnesses and bad outcomes affect us adversely or make us depressed.

Just being a new surgical intern, I recall one of my first nerve-racking experiences when I assisted a surgeon with a patient who had variocele. Varicocele occurs when veins become enlarged inside the scrotum. These veins form a plexus or a cluster near the testicular artery. This can cause fertility problems in men and may retard the growth of one testicle in boys. The only treatment, at that time, was surgery. A one-inch incision is made on the scrotum, and the plexus of veins is removed carefully so that the surgeon does not cut the testicular artery. In addition to myself, the attending was assisted by an anesthesiologist, surgical assistants, and nurses. In the middle of the procedure, the surgeon was called out to look at another more complicated case in a nearby operation theatre. He told me to finish the surgery and then left. I was so inexperienced that I could not differentiate between a vein and an artery! I began to panic; I did not know what to do. I was afraid that the anesthesia would wear off before I could finish. Thankfully, there was no bad outcome, as my attending surgeon returned after fifteen minutes and finished the surgery successfully.

During my medical rounds, I came across a few patients who had leprosy. I had seen people suffering from this disease begging on the street often with missing fingers, toes, or deformed noses. I did not understand how they could bear the suffering while living in abject poverty. The disease was quite prevalent in the sixties with millions of victims, primarily in Asia and Africa. Since then, with prevention efforts by WHO and treatment with medicines such as dapsone, leprosy has declined significantly. Even with these measures, India still has thousands of cases, primarily among the poor and malnourished. While not highly contagious, it can be spread to those living in close contact with lepers by airborne droplet infection, such as from nasal secretions, for instance. Patients develop swellings (granulomas) but since their skin is not sensitive to pain, they develop secondary infections on the untreated wounds. Eventually, the surrounding tissue falls off, causing deformities of extremities. One patient, who came to see us in the early stages, was treated with dapsone and was cured. Another, who had already lost parts of his toes was referred to a surgeon.

I was saddened by the suffering and poverty of the lepers, but glad that I could help in a small way. In the past, there were segregated colonies run by missionaries, most notably Father Damien, a Roman Catholic priest. He treated those infected on the Hawaiian island of Molokai in the 19th century, where a small colony still exists today. He also contracted the disease and died. I also remember hearing about a European surgeon who was treating leprosy patients in a colony in Kerala. Hats off to these people who provide a great service to mankind, often at their own peril. Even though multiple medications are now available to treat and cure this disease in the early stages, half of the world's leprosy cases are found in India.

When I did my obstetrics and gynecology rotation in the sixties, India had a population of approximately half a billion. It was common for a woman to deliver up to six babies. There were multiple reasons; primarily, the lack of knowledge regarding and inability to afford contraception. Millions of people living in poverty and earning less than one dollar a day could not afford to pay for contraceptive devices. This was further complicated by contraception being forbidden by some religions. In addition, because of high infant mortality, a couple produced more babies, thinking that some of them would die. The more they had, the more likely one would survive to care for them when they grew old.

My rotation in public health included preventive medicine and pediatrics. The crippling disease of polio was prevalent in our daily rounds. Patients afflicted with this illness were crippled for life with the inability to walk. I have known a few physicians who have had polio as a child and were left with a severely deformed leg. This did not prevent them from becoming successful doctors and having a happy family life. Polio was declared eradicated in India in 2014 with the help of the polio vaccine.

It was also common to see children with whooping cough, measles, and mumps due to not having the triple DPT (Diptheria, Pertussis, Tetanus) vaccination. Children acquired all sorts of communicable and infectious diseases, but most of them recovered after a few weeks. My cousins and I had chickenpox in school and were told to stay away from other students until we were symptom free. We spent that time in a beautiful bungalow rented by my uncle. It turned out to be a nice vacation.

Since Mangalore did not have a psychiatric hospital, we were required to travel to the larger city of Bangalore to do our one-month rotation. After India's independence in 1948, Bangalore started growing. In the sixties, it attracted defense industries and had an air force base. It was also becoming a major medical center with The National Institute of Mental Health and Neurosciences (NIMHANS) located just outside the city.

The journey to Bangalore was about two hundred miles by winding roads through the Western Ghats. About twenty of us traveled by motorbike and scooter; a two-day journey that was certainly memorable. We took off early in the morning along the narrow, poorly maintained tar roads. We shared the road with cars, trucks, motorbikes, scooters, bullock carts, and pedestrians. In addition, farmers and villagers along the way would walk on the road with their cows, sheep, goats, donkeys, and other livestock. The lorry (truck) drivers were bullies, occupying the middle of the road and approaching at high speed from the opposite direction. When I saw a truck approach, I just had to swerve off the road or be run over.

Besides the driving acrobatics required to navigate these roads on a scooter, you are also subject to the elements of the air. This is intensified by traveling at high speeds. Wearing a jacket provided protection from the cold and wind but was of little help when we drove along stretches of road where thousands of insects would hit us. Luckily, I was wearing glasses. Despite this, I enjoyed the wide-open scenery and the breeze blowing on my face.

We rode in a line, with the motorbikes leading because they had more powerful engines. We usually traveled at 70 mph despite all the dangers on the road. After about fifty miles, we encountered a long climb around dangerous blind curves. I would beep my horn on every corner to let the oncoming traffic know of my presence. The roads were narrow and there would be a steep drop on the side of the road with no side walls or fences protecting us from falling into the valley below. So, we had to be careful. One of my fellow scooter riders did fall about fifteen feet into a small ravine. It was a miracle that he escaped with only a few bruises.

We continued our journey and after about a hundred miles we stopped at a small wayside hotel. Lacking money, about ten of us shared one room. We were dead tired and slept soundly despite being so cramped. The next day we continued, racing with one another. Obviously, the motor bikes were way ahead of us and the scooter drivers struggled to keep up. We had decided to enter the city in one line, trying to impress the local people and make a show. However, when we approached, we all got separated in the heavy traffic. It was getting dark, and having no GPS back then, we relied on directions from a gas station. We finally arrived safely and were ready to start our psychiatry internship.

While I was looking forward to this, I had some mixed feelings. The educational emphasis shifted from learning about the body to learning about the mind. At the time, mental health was not given much priority or significance in India. So, I entered this internship not really knowing what to expect, but with a bit of curiosity and an open mind.

The lectures were given by competent teachers and professors, covering mental illnesses like schizophrenia, manic depressive illness, severe depression and anxiety. One lecturer advised us not to pursue a career in psychiatry unless we were mentally strong and prepared to treat these severe mental illnesses. During the rotation, I began to understand what he meant, as it was difficult to see some of these patients experience such high mental distress. At the same time, it was new and I was fascinated to see patients exhibiting symptoms of schizophrenia, such as hearing voices and experiencing delusions. One patient felt that somebody was after him for no reason at all. Our lecturer presented a patient who thought that he was the Maharaja of Mysore. He was suffering from delusions of grandeur and was manic. Medications like chlorpromazine for schizophrenia, amitriptyline for depression, and lithium for manic depressive illness were available.

Patients who did not respond to medications were subjected to electroconvulsive therapy (ECT). This procedure, best performed under general anesthesia, involves brief electrical stimulation of the brain in order to induce a small seizure. ECT causes changes in brain chemistry that quickly reverse symptoms of certain mental illnesses. In the sixties, ECT was administered without anesthesia at NIMHANS. I saw a male patient brought in by the nurses for a treatment, visibly frightened. He was tied down to the bed with cloth restraints and a mouth guard was inserted to prevent him from breaking his teeth while clenching during a seizure. When he was given the shock, his full body convulsed and he did clench hard. He appeared to be in pain and after a minute or so, he seemed to go into a stupor and was carried back to his ward. Patients could receive up to three such treatments a week for two weeks. With more knowledge over time, the practice of performing ECT without anesthesia and proper medication was eventually declared to be inhumane around the world. Though it was difficult to watch, I did not see any patients being injured at NIMHANS by this procedure. Presently, NIMHANS continues to have a positive reputation and is the apex center for Mental Health and Neuroscience.

During my time off from my psychiatry rotation, I did some sightseeing on my scooter. Bangalore was a beautiful, clean city with gardens, wide streets, little traffic and no pollution. Since that time, Bangalore (now Bengaluru) has grown tremendously. It is one of the five largest cities in India and the streets are heavy with traffic. It is known as the ``Silicon Valley of India" due to the influx of information technology related industries. It is also a center of learning with institutions for the study of medicine, dentistry, law, and the sciences. Just like other large

Indian metropolitan areas, it is a city of contrasts. Here, millionaires reside in fancy houses in rich neighborhoods and poor people reside in slums with inadequate sanitation and other necessary services. Now, these slums are gradually being eradicated and better housing environments are being provided for the poor. Bangalore continues to preserve its rich South Indian heritage and culture by supporting their traditional dancing schools, arts and crafts centers and exhibitions that are unique to the region.

At the conclusion of my year of internship, on January 20, 1968, I was awarded the degree of Bachelor of Medicine and Bachelor of Surgery by Mysore University. I had finally become a doctor. Though I had found psychiatry interesting, at this point in my life, I had no intention of pursuing it in my medical practice. Little did I realize the struggle ahead of me and the direction my path would go in establishing my career.

CHAPTER 6

ENGAGEMENT

With Meena at the Taj Mahal

In 1967, my parents decided that it was time I settled down and married a "good" girl. At that time, it was common in India for couples to become engaged by arrangements made through family and social relationships since dating was not allowed in our community. But, modern India has changed a bit. It is more prosperous and many women have become better educated and are able to make their own living. Therefore, youngsters, both men and women, are more independent and open to nontraditional ways of matchmaking, such as turning to matrimonial websites to find a mate of their own liking.

Regardless of having an arranged marriage or not, the idea that marriages are meant to be forever, remains. Generally speaking, engagements can be broken without too much stigma attached, but divorce is still considered taboo. Until recently, the divorce rate in India was one percent compared to nearly fifty percent in the United States. I do not remember any of my relatives, even in my extended family, being divorced. The marital partners are expected to compromise, adjust and carry on, even though they may not love each other. This may be changing somewhat now since women are more able to leave a bad marriage.

I did get six proposals from parents of girls who were looking for a suitable boy. I informed my father that I wanted to see photographs and get information about all of them and then interview them before deciding. But my parents were determined to let me interview only one girl, of their choosing. That girl turned out to be my wife, Meenakshi, whom I call Meena. Meena's father was also in the umbrella manufacturing business, which was located on the east coast of India in the city of Madras, now known as Chennai. Being in the same field, the parents knew each other, and were from the same socioeconomic, cultural, and religious Jain community. Through our extended family network, my father learned that Meena was a good looking seventeen-year-old and her family had a good reputation in the community. Therefore, he decided that Meena was the right girl for me. My primary criteria, at that age, for choosing a girl was her looks and she more than met that criteria. However, I still insisted on an interview before agreeing to the engagement. My father relented, with the caveat that I could not refuse her unless she had some physical issue, such as, being lame or deaf! Basically, he left me no choice and during those times boys did not go against the wishes of their parents. So, I knew I was "stuck" with this pretty girl and hopefully she would stick it out with me.

Meena was born in the bustling city of Chennai in 1949. Her parents were delighted as a daughter had not been born into the family for a couple of generations. However, from a very young age she was unable to keep in good health. At her grandparents urging, Meena's parents sent her to live with them in Mumbai where the climate seemed to suit her better. It was not uncommon in those days for parents to give in to the wishes of grandparents. She remembers growing up in a loving family environment, spoiled by her doting grandparents and uncles. Our childhoods differed in that way. Although we both came from similar cultural and family backgrounds, I was raised by my parents early on and then moved away from their protective care at the age of eleven. Meena, on the other hand, came back to live with her parents around that age. Though different, we both experienced major life changes early on in our childhoods. These transitions were not of a negative nature, but we both still remember the emotional struggles and adjustments required to adapt to our new lives.

When Meena returned home to live with her parents at age twelve, they lived in a small house in Mylapore, a suburb of Chennai. It was a convenient commute to where her father worked as an honest businessman as part owner of the umbrella factory. Chennai was a big city then and has grown tremendously in the last fifty years. Now, the fifth largest city in India, it is a cultural, economic, and educational center in south India with both modern and traditional values. It is also known as the "Detroit of India" because one third of India's automobile industry is based there. It also attracts many "health tourists" to its large health center.

On a recent trip to Chennai, we were surprised to see how much it had grown in twenty-five years. We visited some of our favorite places, including St. Thomas Church. Its history goes back to 52 A.D. when St. Thomas traveled to India to spread Christianity. It was later rebuilt by the Portuguese and the British. We visited the beautiful Kapaleeshwarar Shiva Temple with its painted idols of Hindu gods. As was customary, I removed my fancy American shoes at the door before entering the Balaji Temple and placed them with the shoes of the other visitors. After I finished praying, I returned to retrieve my shoes and they were gone, despite the watchman standing not too far away. I had to walk barefoot to my car, in the hot sun, and drive to the nearest shoe store to buy a pair of Indian shoes! We also visited our old haunt, the Marina, with its long sandy beach on the Bay of Bengal. In 2015, the BBC ranked Chennai as the hottest city for both visiting and living. Not far from Chennai is the coastal city of Mahabalipuram, where the 7th and 8th century Pallava dynasty kings built magnificent seashore temples and monuments.

During Meena's early teenage years, her maternal uncles and their families also lived in Chennai. She was very close to her cousins and grew up in a happy and fun-loving environment. Our Gujarati Jain business community there was prosperous and owned a lot of businesses. Her uncles had made it big in the glass (spectacles) frame business; manufactured in Chennai and exported to Russia. At that time, exports to Russia were encouraged by the Indian government. They made frequent trips to Russia, taking along many bottles of scotch whiskey, which the Russian bureaucrats and vendors loved. The rule of thumb was to not talk about religion or politics while conducting business in Russia. That way they were able to expand their business and make it successful.

At the time of our engagement, in January 1967, Meena was 17 and I was 23. It was decided that our engagement interview would be held in Mumbai at the Shanmukhananda Hall Hotel, where my parents and I were staying. I knew that our meeting was just a formality. During the meeting I asked her if she had any hobbies and she replied that she liked to collect stamps. Besides that, we did not have much to say to each other. The interview was over in a few minutes. When I emerged from the interview room, my uncle threw a holy coconut at me, which I caught, and then a ceremonial "Chandla " was placed on my forehead and jaggery (brown raw sugar) was put in my mouth; all signifying that I was officially engaged. Nobody asked me whether I liked her or not! I was wondering whether anybody asked her the same about me. After the interview, both of our extended families gathered in one of my uncle's homes to enjoy a feast and come to know each other.

After I got engaged to Meena, I fell in love with her. I had never dated in my life, so this relationship was a new experience for me. There was always much anticipation of when I could see her next. I made a few trips from Mangalore to Chennai during my internship, via train, to visit Meena. I would stay at her parent's home, which was unusual in those days. We were grateful to both our parents that they accepted and allowed these visits. When we were apart, Meena and I would write letters to each other frequently. In this way, our relationship grew. I would write quotes from love songs and poems to her, we would reminisce of our favorite memories from our last visits, and share our longings for the next one.

CHAPTER 7

MEENA

Marriage Ceremony with Meena's Parents By Her Side, 1969

Calicut (Kozhikode), in Kerala state, seemed to be the right place to settle down following my internship, since my parents were there and I was familiar with the city. I felt that I needed some practical experience before establishing my own practice, so my father approached his friend, a well-known general practitioner, who agreed to let me be his assistant.

The general practitioner had his own dispensary, a common practice where liquid mixtures for indigestion, cough or cold, and medications, like sulfadiazine for infection, were dispensed to patients for a fee. Patients with colds, cough, indigestion, constipation, fever, and headaches would flock to the clinic in large numbers and we would provide them with basic medical care. This, along with a post as a senior house officer at the Calicut teaching hospital, I gained much valuable experience.

In the meantime, I was enjoying my time in Calicut. I enjoyed soccer and many major teams from all over India played there. The Nagjee Tournament was sponsored by the umbrella company where my father worked, affording us special seats. It was a prestigious tournament attracting such teams as Bombay Globe, Border Security Force, Rajputana Rifles, Gurkha regiment, Mohammedan Sporting, 515 Air Command and Bangalore Blues. Recreationally, I also enjoyed playing badminton with my relatives, friends and my father.

While I was training under the GP, Meena was attending a college in Chennai. She was in her second year of undergraduate studies, majoring in psychology. I made frequent trips to visit her and became better acquainted with her family. When she would visit her grandparents in Parle, Mumbai, I would accompany my father there on his business trips. On occasion, he would allow me to drive his Fiat in the heavy Mumbai traffic.

One evening, I picked her up and took her to Juhu Beach, an isolated suburb of Mumbai. It was getting dark and we were sitting on the isolated beach enjoying the sea breeze and the soothing sounds of the ocean. Suddenly, we were startled by a man who came up silently behind us, shining his flashlight. He informed us that he was a plainclothes policeman and showed us his badge. After confirming our identities, he told us that the beach was a dangerous place at night; that people had been robbed and even murdered there. We thanked him for the warning and quickly left. As we started to drive off, I noticed a car with several men in it that appeared to be blocking our exit. Suspecting they were a threat, I swerved past them, whereupon they started chasing us. I sped up, reaching speeds of about ninety mph, but they remained close behind. Luckily, the road had little traffic. After a few miles, we reached an intersection where there were more people and they must have stopped chasing us because we lost sight of them. I still believe that Meena and I escaped with our life that evening. The chase reminded me of a scene in the James Bond movie which had just been released in Mumbai. I was proud of myself for being a mini James Bond!

It was during this time that I decided to take my Educational Council for Foreign Medical Graduates (ECFMG) examination in nearby Colombo, Sri Lanka. If successful, I would be allowed to go to the United States to pursue further training, while earning a living. The ECFMG was a grueling, multiple choice examination and my textbook knowledge had faded somewhat. A few weeks after taking the exam, I received notification that I had failed by a small margin. While my hopes were dashed, I was somewhat happy to extend my stay in India, the country I loved.

Meena and I, along with my parents took a car trip to Agra; nearly fourteen hundred miles over narrow roads shared with trucks, cars, bullock carts, bicycles, pedestrians and cattle. We, of course, drove on the left side of the road however, the bullock carts and farmers with cattle did not observe those rules, which made it a challenge to drive safely. We were constantly honking the horn to warn them to get out of the way, with limited success. We had to be especially careful of oncoming trucks that would run us off the road. My father and I took turns driving, not a very pleasant experience. He constantly commented on my lack of driving skills. According to him, I either drove too fast or too slowly. I just could not seem to please him or perhaps he was trying to make me a better driver. With no air conditioning, we had to keep the windows open, and by the time we reached our destination both the car and its occupants were covered in dirt. To top it all off, frequently our car would break down.

On the way, we visited Khajuraho in the central state of Madhya Pradesh. Located four hundred miles south of Delhi, it had been the site of approximately two hundred Hindu and Jain temples, built in the 12th century by Chandela dynasty kings. Over the centuries, these temples were plundered and desecrated until only twenty-five temples remained. They were rediscovered by a British surveyor, T. S. Burt, in 1831. Some of the temples are famous for their erotic sculptures along with numerous other aspects of human life. This attracts many foreign tourists who must surely be impressed by the agility of the ancient Indians depicted performing the "Kama Sutra" sexual exercises! It was a little embarrassing for Meena and me to see these carvings, especially in front of my parents. The inside of the temple, where we went to pray, was decorated with beautiful Hindu deities. This type of architecture was designed to convey the message that one must control the senses, like sexual impulses, before one can meditate and go within to discover divine bliss.

We reached Agra where we visited the famous Taj Mahal, as millions of tourists do every year. It was built by the emperor Shah Jahan in 1653, in memory of his favorite wife, Mumtaz Mahal, who died after giving birth to his 14th child. About two thousand artisans were employed, over twenty years, to build this magnificent example of Mughal architecture. Meena and I were thrilled to visit this monument during our engagement period because it symbolized the eternal love between a man and his wife. I was lucky to have seen so much of India at such a young age and I was thankful to my parents for taking us on this trip.

During our engagement years, Meena and I, along with her parents, traveled by train from Chennai to the hill stations of Nainital and Mussoorie in the northern state of Uttar Pradesh. Nainital was beautiful and we enjoyed the boat rides on the Nainital Lake. Our attempt to get away from her parents to have a few moments by ourselves, were stymied by her mother who would not leave us alone. From Nainital, Meena and I traveled to Clutterbuck Ganj with Meena's Uncle Sharad and Aunt Bhanu. Meena's younger sister, Jyotsna, had also arrived from Chennai to spend a few weeks. Uncle Sharad was a chemical engineer, trained in England, who had recently been hired as a chief manager in a huge camphor manufacturing factory there. They had relocated from Mumbai and were provided a nice home in the company's housing colony.

The only problem was that the colony was inhabited by many monkeys. They were not only intelligent, but quite cunning. Aunt Bhanu would cook a traditional Indian meal for us every day, including chapatis (like tortillas). The monkeys had a habit of coming right into the kitchen and stealing them when Aunt Bhanu's attention was diverted. They also liked her bananas! They would hang around in the ceiling of the house without us knowing. Once, Uncle Sharad was doing his morning yoga exercises, not knowing that a monkey was sitting on the low ceiling above him. As soon as he raised his arms, it caught hold of his hands and would not let them go. He called out to Aunt Bhanu in desperation and she quickly went to the kitchen and threw some chapatis and bananas on the floor. The monkey then let go of Uncle Sharad's hands, grabbed the food, and left the house. After that, my uncle always made sure that a monkey was not around when he did his Hatha Yoga postures! We gradually became accustomed to our pesky ancestors from the animal kingdom. Our non-violent religious beliefs did not allow us to harm them, so we devised methods of preventing them from raiding the house. Eventually, we all lived in peaceful coexistence.

Our wedding date, February 8, 1969, was fast approaching. The ceremony was to be held in Chennai. The wedding party, which included my extended family from Maharashtra, was to reach Chennai by February 7th. They decided to meet in Mumbai and take a five-day cruise on a coal and steam powered mini cruise ship, the 'Sabarmati.' They traveled in first class cabins where they received good service, unlike the third-class passengers who had to sleep on the deck, with minimal facilities. When the ship reached Calicut, it put down anchor about two miles out because the sea was too shallow to enter the harbor. The passengers then transferred to a wooden dhow (sailboat) which took them to the pier where my parents and I met them. The next day, all of us, including my sister, Shobhana, and younger brother, Mukesh, boarded a train bound for Chennai. My one sister, Anupama was living in the United States at the time, so was not able to attend.

When we arrived the next day, we were greeted by Meena's family and taken to the Woodlands Hotel. In those days, Indian weddings were an expensive and elaborate affair with three days of events and feasts. The bride's side of the family bore most of the expense and served as hosts, and Meena's parents did a good job. On the first day we had the "raas garba," a traditional Indian dance. The women were dressed in beautiful sarees and adorned with expensive jewelry. The men wore traditional churidar and kurta dresses. Both men and women danced to the DJ's music, with sticks in their hands.

The wedding was a traditional Hindu ceremony, held at a large wedding venue, "Rajeshwari Kalyana Mandapam." Meena's young uncle, Girish, was married to his bride, Kala, along with us in a dual wedding ceremony. Meena and I circled the ceremonial holy fire seven times and exchanged vows. The priest was chanting Sanskrit prayer versus, called slokas, which none of us understood. He had planned to

RAMESH C. SHAH, MD

chant for about two hours! But having no patience for spending that much time listening to something which I did not understand, I bribed him with some rupees. To our delight, he performed a shorter ceremony! That evening, the reception was held at the same venue. Our family members and friends greeted us, bestowing gifts and blessings.

We spent our honeymoon night in a nearby, fancy hotel suite. One of my unwise friends, in the way of a practical joke, had arranged for a hotel waiter to knock at our suite's door every half hour throughout the night. We quickly grew tired of this and I stood outside the room in a dark corner hoping to catch the perpetrator and knock the hell out of him. I was unable to catch him and calls to the hotel receptionist were fruitless. To this day, I have not found out who arranged this awful prank. The only solace was that we were married and looked forward to a happy life together.

CHAPTER 8

GENERAL PRACTICE

Opening of My Primary Care Clinic In Calicut,
Kerala With Family Giving Their Blessings

The struggle to establish my career still lay ahead of me. So, we settled in Calicut and lived with my parents until we could become financially independent. This living arrangement was somewhat difficult. I had lived in boarding school and hostels most of my life and was independent in my thinking; it was particularly hard for me to adjust. In addition, there was a generational and cultural gap between my parents and us, and we had to follow their rules whether we agreed with them or not. My dad and I both had short tempers, which led to some arguments and hard feelings between us. But we knew that they loved us, and we were thankful to them for providing us food and shelter. My father even bought me an old car to drive back and forth to work. It generally drove well, but during heavy rains, water would seep through the floor and soak my feet. This became untenable, and my father bought me a second-hand Herald car. This car had one minor problem, while driving, the hood would pop open and block my view. This led to some dangerously close shaves until I got it repaired.

We had our share of good times, too. Shobhana, my youngest sister, also lived with my parents and would lighten the atmosphere with her joyful personality and contagious laughter. One evening, she suggested we have dinner at a fancy seaside restaurant. Much to our surprise, after the sumptuous dinner, a scantily clothed woman started dancing seductively in front of us. To make matters worse, she decided to sit on my father's lap. My mother's eyes opened wide with disgust and embarrassment, but she did not say anything. We were all relieved when the dance was over. On the way home, Shobhana started crying. She felt she was to blame for putting our parents in such an uncomfortable position. But Meena and I consoled her, and we all had a big laugh over the experience.

At last, I felt I had enough training to start my own medical clinic. Optimistically, I opened two; one downtown and the other in the nearby semi-rural beach town of Meenchanda. The first obstacle I encountered was the large number of established allopathic medicine general practitioners in Calicut. Patients preferred to go to these well-known, large practices rather than come to an unknown. I was also not fluent in the local language, Malayalam. My difficulty in communicating with my patients caused them to perceive me as an "outsider" and to be concerned that I could not accurately take their medical history. The third challenge was competing with practitioners of alternative medicines, like Ayurveda, homeopathy, and naturopathy, as they did help some patients get better. I also competed against quacks who masqueraded as practitioners, taking advantage of poor and illiterate patients who did not know the difference. Many Indian patients would try different types of alternative practitioners before coming to an allopathic practitioner both because it was more affordable, and they believed that the alternative medications had fewer side effects. We allopathic doctors were a last resort if all else failed. The bottom line was that my practice was not growing as expected. I began to doubt whether I had the knowledge, personality and skills to become a successful general practitioner. But I persevered.

Practicing in the coastal village of Meenchanda proved interesting. I would make house calls to patients who lived in shacks or huts on the beach. In the rainy season I had to wear my knee-high rubber boots because my legs would sink knee deep in the wet sand. Many of the inhabitants were fishermen who often did not have money to pay me. I would accept coconuts or mangoes in payment so as not to offend them. Though I did not make much money, I felt good about helping these patients. I heard stories of unethical doctors who would unnecessarily refer patients to specialists for a kickback who would in turn refer some patients to them. I could never bring myself to do that.

There were days when I waited in my clinic for hours before a patient would show up. But, closing my practice and taking a job in a government-run clinic was not an option. My average pay was around six hundred rupees (80 dollars) per month. Though the rupee went a long way, it was not enough to make a decent living. After a few months, I realized that my ambitious plan to start a successful medical practice was not going to materialize. I could pursue a three year post graduate course in medicine, but I did not know whether I could pass the tough examinations to become a specialist. I was overwhelmed with a sense of urgency for financial independence and seeing no answers to my plight, I went into a state of anxiety and depression. Although I was in the same boat as thousands of Indian college graduates who were not able to find suitable jobs, I felt like a failure. I felt as if my relatives and friends were looking down on me and that I had lost respect at home. I briefly considered becoming a doctor in the Indian armed forces and reside in India. But, I decided to leave India and try my luck abroad.

The United Kingdom (UK) was accepting Indian medical graduates for what they called clinical attachment. I would be assigned to a senior doctor for one month and be assessed for my medical knowledge and competency in English. It would then be decided whether I was fit to stay in the UK and pursue a medical career. However, the waiting period for clinical attachment was long, perhaps a few years. I decided to apply and hope for the best. I again reverted to my high school motto, "never give in." I stopped worrying, and with Meena's support and the strength and hope I found by praying to God, I kept going.

Since I was only busy in my clinics until lunch time each day, I had a lot of time on my hands. I decided to volunteer at the local municipal hospital which served the poor in its numerous inpatient wards. One ward served only patients who were suffering from typhoid fever, which is endemic in India. It is spread by salmonella typhi bacteria from eating food or drinking water contaminated with the feces of an infected person. Many of these patients lived in unsanitary conditions since the city did not have the money to improve their sewage system or water supply. Patients came in with fever and abdominal pain. Without treatment, the infection could spread to the rest of the body, causing ulcers in the intestines and attacking other organs. It rarely led to death. During my house calls, I had treated a few patients with antibiotics and advised them to rest. While making rounds, a nurse would follow me with a bowl of antiseptic lotion. After examining the patient, I would dip my hands in the bowl and then move on to the next patient. This way I would not catch the infection myself or pass it on. Patients with minimal symptoms could become chronic carriers of the disease. The typhoid vaccine, along with improved sanitary conditions and prevention efforts, has resulted in the incidence of typhoid decreasing in India.

I would spend a few hours in the outpatient department. I would sit at a table with my prescription pad and a stethoscope while a large number of patients surrounded me; each trying to get me to listen to his or her complaints and write them a prescription. Many had common complaints such as colds, coughs or indigestion. It was especially sad to see impoverished, malnourished women waiting for a long time with a crying child in their arms. Some had multiple children and seemed to be in a never-ending cycle of misery. Educating couples regarding birth control would be one of the answers to controlling the population which, in turn, would alleviate some of the hardships.

I saw a woman die after an unsuccessful abortion attempt by an unscrupulous quack who inserted a stick in her uterus to kill the fetus. He had perforated her uterus, resulting in grave complications. Malpractice was unheard of then, and to my knowledge he was never prosecuted.

The government used to incentivize men to have a vasectomy by handing out transistor radios. Despite these efforts, India's population continued to explode. Even today, despite India's growing economy, twenty five percent of the population lives on less than two dollars a day and a high percentage of these children are undernourished.

I knew that this was my last chance to treat indigent Indian patients before I left for the UK. So, I continued to volunteer my services without pay. There were also countless doctors who were underpaid, but continued to work in these hospitals and in remote areas. American billionaire, Bill Gates, and former presidents, Bill Clinton and Jimmy Carter, understand the plight of the people in third world countries. They are continuing their efforts, and along with international and American aid, are making progress in eradicating disease in these countries.

I spent a few months volunteering my services at Marikunnu Hospital on the outskirts of Calicut. There was a beautiful statue of Mother Mary on the grounds and the hospital was staffed by the Ursiline Sisters of Mary Immaculate. It was inspiring to see these European and Indian nurses dedicating their lives to Jesus Christ through service to others. These experiences instilled a spirit of service and compassion in me that I hoped to continue in my life when working with underprivileged patients.

CHAPTER 9

CALICUT, KERALA

My Father (tallest man next to tree) and Me (behind
woman in saree) at a 'Lions Club Free Milk Center'
Providing Food for the Poor Children

While I continued with my practice and my volunteer work, I started preparing for my potential clinical attachment by reading the "Textbook of Medicine" by Cecil and Loeb every evening. I wanted to make a good impression when I reached the UK. Meena had finished two years of college and was keeping house with my mother and dealing with her idiosyncrasies. We were all still trying to adjust to each other's temperaments, which required work on everyone's part. They often visited the local Jain Temple to pray and socialize. Otherwise, Meena's life was pretty routine, including cooking vegetarian food for the family.

Many advancements in the running of the kitchen and house has happened since then. During her younger days, my mother cooked on a coal stove. After that, cooking was done on a gas burning "primus stove" that is sometimes still used today when camping. Later on, small gas cylinders were brought to the kitchen and attached to the stove to provide gas heat. Another change was in how we bathed. In my younger days, the hot water for bathing was heated in a barrel over a wood fire. It was later replaced by electric hot water heaters that were mounted to the wall.

While my mother and Meena were taking care of the home front and I was busy trying to further my medical career, my father managed the umbrella factory and was very active in the Lion's Club, serving as both president and deputy district governor. The Lions are an international organization dedicated to, among other things, creating and fostering "a spirit of understanding among the peoples of the world" and taking "an active interest in the civic, cultural, social and moral welfare of the community." During my stay in Calicut, I was happy to participate in some of the Lions Club community activities with my father, such as serving free milk to the poor children of the area. Another one of their principal charities deals with serving the visually impaired and blind. During my father's involvement, there were thousands of Indians suffering from cataracts who could not afford the surgery. The Lions arranged for Dr. Modi to conduct an "eye camp" where patients would receive the surgery free of charge. Hundreds of patients lined up and he would examine them one day and perform surgery the next. The nurses would then provide antibiotics, bandage the eye, provide a pair of glasses, and advise the patient to follow up with their family doctor. I, along with others, assisted in one of these camps. We went from patient to patient making sure that they did not develop post-surgical complications, such as, infection. Over the years, the Lions helped thousands of grateful Indian patients regain their eyesight.

Impressed with my father's zeal for service, I joined the Junior Chamber of Commerce (Jaycees), a service and leadership organization for young professionals. I attended a South India Junior Chamber convention where multiple clubs had gathered. I took part in the debating competition and took first place. My public speaking training in Lawrence school came in handy. I became more confident in this skill, which helped later in my career.

When 1973 arrived, I had been out of medical college for five years and I still had not established a successful practice. I had not heard from the UK regarding a clinical attachment and my patience was wearing thin. My frustration was compounded by feelings of sadness and anxiety. I visited a nearby Balaji temple for a blessing and a prayer to God that my wishes might be granted soon.

I finally did get a call for clinical attachment that spring. Meena was pregnant with our first child and had gone to her parents' home, per Indian custom, to await the delivery. Our daughter, Shefali, was born in August. I waited until she was born. In September, I decided to go alone to England to start my clinical attachment and prepare for my family's arrival. I believed Shefali had brought this lucky break to my life. I did not wish to leave my beloved India and my family, but it looked as if my destiny lay in the west. When the day of my departure arrived, many of my extended family members came to the Mumbai airport to see me off. They put garlands around my neck and wished me luck. I was grateful for their love for me and our family. I did not realize how many obstacles lay ahead.

CHAPTER 10

ENGLAND

Departing for London from Mumbai Airport, 1973

I arrived in London on a cold September morning. As I was going through Customs and Immigration, I could see that we Indians were treated differently. The British personnel were speaking rudely to some older Indians who had just arrived on a flight from Africa. With my two bags in hand, I took a bus to meet up with an acquaintance of my father, who was to guide me around London. I waited for an hour, but he did not show up. I had made arrangements to stay in the central London YMCA, so I decided to go alone. As soon as I stepped out, two cabbies came to me asking if I wanted a ride. They seemed shady, so I decided to take the underground train from a nearby tube station. London had fewer people than Mumbai and the streets were cleaner; I hardly saw any trash on the roads. The cars drove on the left side of the road, as they did in India, but the traffic was orderly with hardly any honking. Of course, there were more white faces and people barely talked with each other. I noticed many of them carried umbrellas in anticipation of the frequent London rain. Adjoining old buildings lined the streets and some areas had cute little shops and restaurants.

That had been my first experience in an underground tube train, and I was impressed with both the fact that there was no locomotive and that we arrived on time. I disembarked after a few stops and walked one mile to the YMCA. My suit pants were too big at the waist and I was trying to hold them up while carrying the two suitcases. As luck would have it, it started raining heavily and I was quickly drenched. A man passed by remarking, "Oh, my!" in his English accent, offering no help. When I arrived, seeing my plight, the receptionist was kind enough to assign me a room right away. After a hot shower to rejuvenate me, I found vegetarian food in the cafeteria, enough to satisfy my appetite, and I hit the bed. My first day in London had at least ended well.

I was ready to start my one-month clinical attachment at Orpington Hospital, in Kent County, about 20 miles out of London. Orpington was a small British town with clean streets and an upper middle class predominantly white population. I was given a small one room apartment with an attached bath on the hospital campus. I met Dr. Gillin, my senior doctor, who seemed to be from the old British school. The next day he assigned me to clinical rounds with his assistant, Dr. Talby, a tall, handsome English internist. He was friendly and a good doctor. After examining a patient, he would ask me questions regarding the patient's symptoms and diagnosis. After getting a satisfactory answer he would proceed to explain the appropriate treatment. He was impressed with my knowledge of internal medicine and satisfied with my fluency in English.

The hospital itself was clean and well equipped. The wards were not as crowded as the municipal hospital in India. Patients were treated well and with courtesy by the staff. I soon learned some English etiquette and manners. I learned not to interrupt while someone was talking, and to wait my turn before asking a question. I was using the words "please" and "thank you" more often. I also learned to request permission from a patient before examining them, gently. Human life was highly valued there, and everything had to be done to save a patient's life. Strict hygienic precautions were observed, and I hardly saw any tropical diseases. Instead I saw cases of lung, heart ailments and neurological problems. I enjoyed doing rounds with Dr. Talby. All the senior doctors were white Englishmen, and in the dining room, they all would sit at one table. The junior, mostly Indian doctors, would sit at another. It seemed to be an unwritten rule.

October passed quickly and Dr. Talby was satisfied with my performance. He wrote me a letter of reference stating that my knowledge of medicine and English was satisfactory and that I was qualified to stay in the UK and undergo training. Without that reference, I would have had to return to India. I had crossed my first obstacle.

I wasted no time in getting a certificate of temporary registration as a medical practitioner from the General Medical Council's Office in London. With an eye toward specializing in internal medicine, I applied for jobs as a senior house officer all over England. I lined up a handful of interviews for jobs which were advertised in journals like the British Medical Journal. I traveled by train, staying in quaint British inns. Everywhere I went, the competition was stiff, with about seven candidates for each job. I was not successful in these interviews and I was getting low on cash. I was getting desperate and would take any job, anywhere to survive.

My long-term plan was to get a MRCP, Member of the Royal College of Physicians, degree from the UK and then, possibly return to India where specialists enjoyed a good life. Finding it difficult to get a job in internal medicine, I started applying for jobs in other fields, including psychiatry. I chose psychiatry since those jobs were less demanding and I would have spare time to study for the Educational Council for Foreign Medical graduates (ECFMG). Passing this examination would give me an opportunity to migrate to the US if I chose. British medical graduates were looking for greener pastures and were migrating to Australia, New Zealand, Canada and Europe. This caused a shortage of doctors in the United Kingdom which was filled by candidates from third world countries, like me. Eventually, I received a call for an interview from a hospital in Wales. It was an old hospital with medical, surgical and OB/GYN units. It had a free-standing building which housed the inpatient psychiatric unit and outpatient psychiatric offices. I was interviewed for the job of Senior House Officer in Psychiatry and got the job for one year. Little did I know that I was to embark on a new career.

CHAPTER 11

WALES

Senior House Officer in Psychiatry

The Welsh were friendly people and their English accent was different from the people living in England. Many were coal miners who from time to time would go on strike for better wages. We could sense the dislike the labor class had for the rich upper class. Since Wales did not produce enough doctors in the seventies, many of their senior hospital staff came from England and Scotland. The junior physicians were primarily from Wales, England, India and the Middle East. There was one American who was friendly and described to us what it was like to practice medicine in the States. We liked his American accent. We came to know each other well, meeting in the doctor's lounge, morning and afternoon, for tea complete with pastries and biscuits. Those from the Middle East countries were hilarious and friendly.

My senior, the registrar in psychiatry, was from India. He showed me the ropes of the psychiatric units, which were segregated by gender, and also had a locked unit for agitated patients. The units were managed by both male and female Welsh nurses. I learned about psychiatric illnesses like depression, anxiety, schizophrenia, manic depressive illness (bipolar illness), alcohol abuse, and how to manage them, mostly with psychiatric medications. We alternated night calls consulting with the emergency room doctor regarding difficult psychiatric patients. Though I would come to an accurate diagnosis and knew the appropriate treatment, I would call my attending to confirm that I was correct, a reflection, perhaps, of my insecurities and anxiety. My attending psychiatrists were knowledgeable, experienced, and taught us well.

One of my first patients, Susan, had symptoms of major depression; insomnia, loss of appetite, lack of motivation, feeling blue and inability to function. She did not have active suicidal plans and promised not to harm herself. She was treated with first generation antidepressants, i.e. tricyclics antidepressants. She was advised of the potential side effects (weight gain, dry mouth and drowsiness). She understood and consented to treatment. She had only mild side effects and I saw her frequently to assure that she did not hoard her antidepressant in order to take a lethal overdose. She was referred to a counselor to help deal with her stressors which included considering divorcing her husband and financial problems. After two months of treatment, her depression started to lift. She regained her appetite, her marriage improved, and she was motivated to perform her daily chores. I continued to see her on an outpatient basis and was impressed that psychiatric medication, along with counseling, did bring about remarkable improvement.

Another patient, William, whose severe depression was not responding to two different trials of antidepressants and counseling, was also having suicidal ideation. He was not able to work and thus, had a hard time paying his bills and supporting his family. One of the attending psychiatrists recommended ECT (electro convulsive therapy) under anesthesia. After a course of ECTs, William had mild memory loss which later resolved itself. He was pleased with the result and eventually went back to work, to the delight of his family. Some of the patients, with a history of severe recurrent depression, needed continued treatment for years to keep their depression in remission. Administering ECTs to severely depressed patients was quite common in the UK at that time. I gave ECTs, with the help of an anesthesiologist, to a row of patients with a mobile ECT machine. I enjoyed treating these patients, witnessing firsthand that depression was treatable and that we were improving people's lives.

Kevin was a particularly neurotic patient with severe anxiety, psychosomatic problems and relationship issues with his wife. He would not reveal his past traumatic history, which may have had a bearing on his condition. One of my attending psychiatrists decided to give him intravenous pentothal. He went into a deep trance and upon questioning started narrating details regarding his past. The attending gave him suggestions to improve his symptoms while he was under deep trance and was able to provide him insights during psychotherapy sessions.

Over a course of a few psychotherapy sessions, Kevin did become less anxious and his relationship with his wife improved.

Shawn, a heavy abuser of alcohol, was not able to abstain, despite psychotherapy. He had been cited for driving under the influence and was missing work. His wife and family were very supportive of his seeking treatment. On the advice of my attending, we decided to treat him with Antabuse, a drug that would cause the patient to have heart palpitations and vomit if they drank alcohol in any form. To demonstrate the effect on his body, we gave him a tablet, and he voluntarily drank a very small amount of alcohol. He started throwing up, his heart started beating fast and he became very uncomfortable. After this unpleasant experience, he never again touched alcohol. He took the Antabuse daily while continuing his course of psychotherapy. He was a highly motivated and intelligent patient. He attended AA meetings regularly, remained abstinent from alcohol, and became a productive member of society to the delight of his family. He was happy with the outcome.

Obtaining a driver's license in Wales proved a challenge, though I had taken lessons from a driving instructor. Driving on the left side of the road was familiar, since I drove on the left side in India, but in Great Britain they observed strict speed limits, something not done in India. Parallel parking was difficult to master, but necessary since most of the cars were parked close together on the side of the road. I failed this part the first two times. The examiner informed me right away that I was unsuccessful. I was always polite and took the news calmly. One of my colleagues was not so calm, yelling at the examiner after hearing that he had failed. Thereafter, he was repeatedly failed by the examiners. After my third attempt, I obtained my driver's license. I bought a small green British car, similar to a Mini Cooper.

Meena joined me in February of 1974, leaving Shefali alternately in the care of her parents for a few months and then mine. She could not have brought her to Wales because we were still not settled, and I was not making enough money. Leaving her behind was very difficult. When Meena arrived at the London airport she was wearing a saree and had waist long hair; she was very pretty. Within a few days of her arrival she cut her hair and switched to pants and a top, more suitable for the Welsh climate. She had a difficult time adapting to the cold and wet weather and we had to buy warm clothes for both of us, which we could barely afford.

We rented a two-story house a few miles away from the hospital. The lower floor had a big living room with a coal burning fireplace where we slept many nights since it was the only room that got enough heat. The house was heated by a series of pipes containing water, heated by the coal burning fireplace.

The only vegetarian food the hospital cafeteria served was mostly salads and potatoes. I was getting fed up with eating that every day. The nearest Indian grocery store was a few hours away, but we would make the trip so that we could cook Indian food at home. To supplement my meager salary, Meena found a job at a nearby cemetery, selling plots and tombstones. This extra income allowed us to make trips to the beautiful Welsh countryside along the mountainous winding roads.

In the evening we enjoyed shows on our black and white TV. This was our first experience with watching television, since India did not have it, and we enjoyed even the limited programming. We especially liked the British comedy shows. We could also watch the American shows "Cannon" and "The Streets of San Francisco," but we felt they erroneously depicted the US as a place of violence and unrest. We knew that it was a better place and our eventual destination. I did not want to return to India since I had no post graduate degree and knew that Britain was not the place where we wanted to settle down. There, we sometimes felt like second class citizens. Britain had national health service and most of the lower paying jobs went to Indians while the higher paying jobs went to the British. Besides, we were not thrilled with the climate.

I still had to pass the ECFMG examination if I wanted to move to the US. I started studying medical textbooks and ECFMG guidebooks again. It had been five years since I passed my MBBS exam in India, and four years since I was unsuccessful in my first attempt at the ECFMG in Sri Lanka. My medical knowledge had become rusty. But, I kept slogging through and made a second attempt at the ECFMG examination in London. Frustratingly, I was unsuccessful again. However, I decided to try one more time. After a few weeks, I got the news that I had passed! Meena and I were delighted that I now had another option. In the meantime, I was getting more experience in psychiatry and starting to like it.

CHAPTER 12

SCOTLAND

At Loch Lomond With Family

When my appointment was not renewed after the first year, I started looking for a job in psychiatry anywhere in the United Kingdom. I was beginning to doubt that I would find a job, when I got an interview call from Hartwood Hospital in Scotland. To reach Hartwood, I had to drive to Liverpool and take a train to Glasgow. I would then stay overnight in Glasgow and the next day take another train to the interior of Scotland. Unfortunately, before I could reach Liverpool, the brakes on my car gave out. In addition, the car was also making an unusually loud noise. I managed to get to a gas station with a mechanic and explained the car's problem. I told him that I had only an hour to catch the train to Glasgow and he agreed to drop me off at Liverpool station. I told him that I would leave the car to be repaired and pick it up when I returned. I was used to roughing it on Indian trains, traveling in overcrowded third-class compartments with inadequate toilet facilities, but this train had very few passengers. I enjoyed the comfortable ride to Glasgow while traveling through the beautiful English countryside and into the hills of Scotland. I hired a taxi to drive around Glasgow, hoping to find a room, but there was a Libertarian convention in town and the hotels were full. So, the taxi driver took me to the outskirts of Glasgow, and to my relief, I found a bed and breakfast. I was exhausted after a long and eventful day and fell fast asleep. Next day, after a sumptuous breakfast, I boarded a train at Glasgow's large and impressive railway station. I had seen photographs of World War II British soldiers boarding trains in this station on their way to war. We passed several towns on the way and I was getting anxious regarding the remote location of the hospital.

Finally, I arrived at Shotts Station from where I took a short ride to the hospital, which was in the middle of nowhere. It looked like a huge medieval castle with twin towers. I went to the main office and waited for my interview with the Chief Psychiatrist and Administrator. I had anticipated more candidates for the position, and was pleased that with no competition the job was probably mine. The administrator was a tall slim Scotsman with a pleasant demeanor and an accent distinctly different from either the Welsh or the English. I had to listen closely to fully understand what he was saying. He told me about the history of the hospital, which opened in 1890. In the 70s it housed more than a thousand patients, about half of which were geriatric, some suffering dementia. The other half were younger and suffered from common psychiatric illnesses (schizophrenia, manic depressive illnesses, alcoholism, substance abuse, depression, and anxiety). The hospital had several buildings with wards spread over at least half a mile. When I was taken on a tour of the hospital, I was overwhelmed by its sheer size and the number of patients it housed. The chief psychiatrist introduced me to a few of the Scottish consultants and a few junior Indian doctors. I was offered the job and accepted readily.

I picked up my mini from Liverpool, thanked the good mechanic, and headed home. Meena and I were sad to leave Wales and the wonderful friends we had made. But, we were looking forward to our next adventure in Scotland.

The hospital provided an apartment in an old Victorian style building on the grounds. We were greeted by the seven junior Indian doctors on our arrival, some of whom were married with children. They helped us unload our luggage and were happy to have another junior psychiatrist on staff to help with their heavy patient workload.

The staff consisted of eight Scottish and two Indian consultants, experienced and knowledgeable in treating psychiatric patients, who came each morning to do rounds. Each supervised two wards with the assistance of a junior doctor and a nurse. They would finish around lunchtime, leaving the patients under our care. Our shift would end at 4pm and we would then rotate calls among ourselves.

Initially, it caused me some anxiety to take calls and be responsible for so many patients. Soon I gained more confidence and experience in treating psychiatric patients in crisis. The nurses were proficient and would call us only in case of emergencies, such as when an alcoholic patient became aggressive or mildly psychotic. They were given an injection called "combined," a combination of an antipsychotic and a sedative. The hospital staff helped me learn and treat patients with a variety of psychiatric illnesses including severe depression, schizophrenia, anxiety disorders, bipolar disorder, alcoholism and dementia.

The size of the campus made it difficult to walk to all the wards, so I would have to drive from one to another. Some were locked to prevent agitated or suicidal patients from leaving. Some of our patients had been there for years. I gradually got used to their accent, as they did mine, so that I could take a decent psychiatric history. I was glad to see some of them improve over a few weeks.

During our leisure hours, Meena and I traveled to Glasgow and Edinburgh. Once a month we would have a party in the evening. Our wives would cook some tasty vegetarian snacks. Our new Scottish friends would bring their own food. Once they brought a favorite known as haggis, a savory pudding. It is made of sheep's heart, liver, lungs, minced onion, oatmeal, suet, spices and salt mixed with stock. Traditionally, it is encased in an animal's stomach, but this time it was in an artificial casing. But we just ate our vegetarian food. The Scots enjoyed their Scotch, manufactured only in Scotland and famous the world over. Our favorite alcoholic drinks consisted of Portuguese wine, Scotch and European beer. The party would last late into the night, with those of us who were on call abstaining from drinking.

Scotland has long daylight hours in summer and long nights in winter. The winters were somewhat depressing, with rain, wind, and snow. The long and lively Christmas holiday season was a great respite. During our hospital staff parties, there would be singing of carols and dancing. Some of the nurses would carry a small bottle of Scotch in their back pocket which they share with us. We in turn would share ours with them. The natives seemed to have a high tolerance for drinking. I drank minimally but enjoyed the snacks and cookies. I appreciated the comradery of the Scots and their culture.

Meena and I remember our first trip into Edinburgh, the capital. It is a medieval city with beautiful Georgian New Town in its center. There are elegant neoclassical mansions, squares, terraces, and gardens with Holyrood Park overlooking the city of Edinburgh. As we approached, snowflakes started falling on Edinburgh Castle, making it appear like something out of a fairytale. It was my first experience of snow and I will never forget that sight. We visited a museum inside the castle with memorabilia from the British Empire. One of the rooms had an exhibit of the armor worn by Tipu Sultan of South India. This brave king was defeated by a British regiment in the battle of Srirangapatnam Fort in 1799. The regiment consisted mostly of young soldiers from Scotland. At the time, the British empire extended from India to Africa, Egypt, Saudi Arabia, West Indies, and even to Guyana and Belize in South America. It was mind boggling to think how the British sailed thousands of miles from their home shores to build the empire. By the 18th century, Britannia truly ruled the seas (waves).

The Scottish parliament building is in the Holyrood park area. While it has some legislative powers, it is part of the UK. Queen Elizabeth has a residence in Scotland (Balmoral Castle) and her husband is the Duke of Edinburgh, an honorary title.

During one of our visits, we saw the traditional Scottish pipe band wearing their traditional kilts, marching in a parade. The harp was the national instrument of Scotland until it was replaced by the pipe in the 15th century. We also saw traditional Scottish folk dance performed by men and women wearing kilts, dancing to a fast tempo. The rumor is that the men usually do not wear underwear underneath their kilts. So, they were careful not to kick their legs too high! Meena and I enjoyed all of it immensely.

During spring, Meena and I went to see the Loch Ness in the Scottish Highlands; it is the largest freshwater lake in the UK. Legend has it that a large animal, similar to a dragon or dinosaur, inhabits the lake. This animal is known as the Loch Ness monster or "Nessie." There have been numerous reported sightings since 1933. However, the scientific community feels that there is no proof and that the sightings and photographs are hoaxes. We took a cruise on the lake and I had my camera out, just in case. But, to our disappointment, we did not see Nessie.

Scotland also provided me with my first attempt at skiing, on Aviemore ski slopes. I could not get my balance and kept falling on the snow again and again. Each time I would fall, two big Scottish female nurses would come to my rescue. Each one would take an arm and yank me up. Needless to say, this was a humiliating experience and I was lucky to escape with only a few scrapes, bruises and a sore back. On the way back the staff gave me a peg of whiskey and sang hilarious Scottish songs to cheer me up. I did try to smile.

By the spring of 1974, Meena and I had decided to leave Scotland and settle down in the US. I was eligible to start a residency training program in July 1975, so I started applying for psychiatry residency spots all over the US. I wanted to finish my residency and land a suitable job with reasonable pay as soon as possible. Though I might have liked to get a residency in fields such as dermatology, I knew those residency spots were hard to find. I was thirty years old and had the responsibility of supporting my wife and child. Since I already had some training and practical experience in psychiatry, I decided on that field. I lined up interviews in Kansas City, Newark, Louisville, Norfolk, Washington, DC, and Wilmington, Delaware. My younger sister, Anupama, had immigrated with her husband to Dayton, Ohio in the late sixties, so I decided to stay with them and take flights to the interviews.

The hospital in Newark offered the possibility of paying for my travel from Scotland. So, I packed up and took a flight from Glasgow to New

York, and then a bus to Newark. After watching "Cannon" and "Kojak," I was a bit apprehensive about crime. I checked into a downtown motel, locked my door, and decided to settle down for the night. I was kept awake by the constant sirens of police cars and ambulances. This type of noise raised my anxiety level as I started suspecting that the area was probably dangerous. The next morning, after a restless night, I took a taxi to the hospital. The interviewers did not seem particularly enthusiastic about me and I was not offered the job.

As I proceeded through my interviews, I became quite good at it. The administrator at one of the hospitals offered me a residency but would not file for "sixth preference visa." This process required the employer to send a letter to the US National Immigration Agency stating that there was a shortage of psychiatrists in the US and that I was needed to reduce that shortage. Upon acceptance of the sixth preference, I could get a green card allowing me and my family to stay permanently. Since I had no intention of returning to India or the UK, this became a 'must have' for me. I returned to Dayton frustrated and anxious about the possibility that I might not find a suitable residency spot.

During my stay, I learned that Ohio State University (OSU) Hospital, in nearby Columbus, had a psychiatry residency program. I was interviewed and then returned to Dayton to wait; but the OSU residency director did not call. In the meantime, I was offered a residency in Louisville, Kentucky. So, I called OSU demanding a decision or I would accept the position in Louisville. He offered me the position and agreed to sponsor me for the sixth preference visa. OSU was a reputable university and I was happy to get a residency there.

I said goodbye to my sister and returned to Scotland. It was time for us to be reunited with our daughter who was nearly two years old. We both missed her but being away from Shefali was especially hard on Meena, making her sad and moody. My parents agreed to bring her to London in April 1975. They arrived safely and when they deplaned my mother was carrying Shefali, who looked cute and wore a chandla (a small round ornamental dot) on her forehead. She stared at us but clung to my mother who was known to her. We all began the road trip to Scotland, with Shefali in the back of our small economy Mini car. All went well, except whenever I sped up, Shefali would start screaming, and whenever I slowed down, she would quiet. After a while, not used to this, I could no longer take her wailing and I pulled over. I yelled at her to be quiet and that she would be fine! I don't know whether she understood, but she quieted down and we passed through the Scottish Highlands in relative silence.

Our daughter started spending more time in Meena's care and less with my mother. This was necessary to transition her to Meena since my parents were leaving for Dayton in a month's time. After a few days, she started sleeping in the same bed with her. Shefali felt the motherly love and affection that Meena was showering on her and gradually became attached to her.

During the summertime, Scotland's daylight hours extend until near midnight. My mother had difficulty sleeping even though we had covered our windows with black drapes. When my parents left for Dayton, we took Shefali to the Shotts train station near Hartwood and showed her the trains departing. We told her that my parents had taken one of those trains and had gone far away and would not be back. She bought that story and settled down with us without much fuss.

By May 1975, I had resigned my position at Hartwood, explaining that I had accepted a position in the United States. When I informed my junior Indian colleagues that I was leaving, some of them tried to convince me otherwise; even telling me stories about Indian doctors being mugged in the streets. But that did not deter me. We said our goodbyes to our Scottish consultants, junior Indian doctors and the Scottish nurses. We had become attached to these people and it was hard for us to say goodbye. With resolve we left Scotland to start a new life just like countless immigrants had done before us.

Skiing in Aviemore, Scotland

CHAPTER 13

THE OHIO STATE UNIVERSITY
USA

With Shefali at University Arms Apartments

When we arrived in Ohio, our first priority was to find an apartment compatible with my $7000 a year salary and within a reasonable commute to work. We were fortunate to find a 2-bedroom unit near the university with a Montessori school nearby for Shefali. Some of my fellow first year residents also lived there, so we had company. I bought a secondhand Ford Maverick, a two-door sedan with good horsepower. Meena went to school to learn data processing and babysat for our neighbors in her spare time. She would drop me off at Upham Hall psychiatric department, then take Shefali to school before proceeding to her place of employment. In the evening, while I read my psychiatry books, she would cook and play with Shefali. Life was stressful and hectic, but we managed.

The OSU campus is situated near downtown, a huge sprawling complex with multiple buildings spread over 1600 acres, the third largest university campus in the US. It has an enormous library and about 1200 student organizations. Its colleges of engineering, business, law, public affairs, dentistry and medicine have seen thousands of alumni go on to prominent careers. I was proud to be a part of such an illustrious university. The psychiatry department was located in Upham Hall, a multistoried building which housed the inpatient adult and children's psychiatric wards, the psychology department, a lecture hall and several physicians' offices.

On my first day of residency, I was introduced to my fellow residents, a mix of American and foreign medical graduates and to our attending psychiatrists and professors. At that time, psychiatry was not a popular specialty among American medical graduates. This was partly because psychiatrists did not make as much money as the other specialties like surgery, cardiology and neurology. So, this gap in psychiatry residency slots was filled by foreign medical graduates, many of whom did not have a choice, because the first preference for the better paying specialties usually went to American medical graduates. I was one of the lucky ones, I liked psychiatry.

The busy work schedule was a bit of a shock to my system. I had just arrived from Scotland, where the work schedule was light and somewhat laid back, interrupted by tea breaks during the day. Our work at OSU started at 8am with morning rounds, accompanied by the attending psychiatrist. Our lunch was a" brown bag" affair during which we listened to lectures. The psychiatry staff consisted of psychiatrists, psychologists, social workers, licensed counselors and nurses. This staff was highly knowledgeable and experienced and I was getting good training under them. The afternoons were spent in the outpatient department. Many of these counseling and medication management sessions were recorded. My supervising psychiatrist and I would listen to the tape afterward and he would offer me valuable advice on the art of psychotherapy. I was also on a rotating call schedule to attend to psychiatric emergencies on the psychiatric and medical wards, as well as the emergency room. These calls required me to sleep in the department's doctor's room so that I would be readily available. I gradually adjusted to this hectic schedule. On occasion, my big mouth and attitude got me into trouble with the staff by inadvertently rubbing them the wrong way. However, my attendings gave me good advice and guidance. It helped me to grow and get along better with the staff. I was thankful to them.

* * *

One night when I was on call, I was asked to evaluate a psychiatric patient in the emergency room. He seemed quite agitated and was wondering why he had been brought there. He was a young white male in his second year at a nearby college. His father told me that his son's grades had steadily fallen and that he had ended his studies because he had difficulty concentrating and getting along with others. He had become less sociable and kept to himself playing his guitar. His grooming had deteriorated, sometimes he would not shower for days at a time. When he was watching a TV soap opera, he felt that some of the characters were talking to him. He had stopped answering the phone believing that people were threatening him. During the interview with him, he said he was hearing voices and that some of them were making derogatory comments about him. His appetite was fair, but his sleep was disturbed. He claimed that he did not want to harm himself or anyone else but was getting more agitated. He drank only occasionally; however, admitted he was considering drinking more to reduce his agitation and relieve boredom. His father said that the boy's mother had a psychotic episode when she was young, but that his son had no history of psychiatric illness. The patient was physically healthy, and his labs and drug screen were normal. I made the diagnosis of schizophrenia paranoid type based on his history and presenting clinical symptoms. They both consented to the treatment.

I ordered a shot of an antipsychotic to lessen his agitation and hospitalized him for a few days in the psychiatric ward. He gradually improved with antipsychotic medication and counseling. The voices had stopped, and he was much less paranoid and delusional. He was discharged a few days later under his parent's care with a recommendation for counseling regarding his daily activities and relationships. After a few months, he still had not returned to college, but was getting along better with people. His thinking continued to be slow and he had difficulty expressing his emotions. However, he was socializing more and was starting to learn a trade. The family was satisfied with his progress.

*   *   *

Winters in Columbus were severe. One such winter brought a blizzard which lasted for three days. People were advised not to travel on the icy roads and the temperatures were below zero with strong and howling winds. With visibility at less than five yards due to the blowing snowfall, a person could die from exposure if stranded. I happened to be on call all three days, by myself, because other residents were trapped in their homes and could not drive to work. I prayed that I would not be confronted by too many psychiatric emergencies at one time.

During that night I was called to see a patient in the emergency room who had been brought in by the police. A white male had taken an overdose of sedatives and had been found in a semi-conscious condition by his family. The patient's stomach was pumped, and he was given intravenous fluids and revived. I proceeded to take the patient's history. He was having marital problems and had been fired from his job. He was despondent and had resorted to alcohol, which made him more depressed. He eventually took an overdose of a relative's sedatives, hoping to die in his sleep. I talked to him about his stressors and did a suicide assessment. This had not been his first suicide attempt and he had a long history of depression. Based on this, I admitted him to the locked psychiatric unit with his agreement. I gently encouraged him that with courage and patience he would be able to face his stressors and start a new life. His treatment plan included cognitive behavior psychotherapy, an antidepressant, and abstinence from alcohol that was assisted by a medication to reduce his craving. After about ten days, he no longer felt suicidal and was discharged under the care of one of his relatives. We had weekly follow-up appointments to monitor his progress and he was also advised to attend Alcoholics Anonymous meetings for at least a year, which he promised. He had stopped drinking. Within a few weeks, he came out of his depression and found a job. He was also attending marital counseling sessions with his wife and their relationship was improving. He thanked me for my help. I was gaining some valuable experience in treating difficult psychiatric patients. Many of them improved with treatment and were able to regain a higher level of functioning. This was gratifying and it made me feel good that we were able to help these patients.

My challenge now was to pass another examination so that I could become a licensed physician in the US. The FLEX exam was one such test and it was very difficult to pass. If I failed, I would have to get another job, perhaps a lab technician or a pharmacy tech. I did not want to be in that predicament, nor did I wish to go back to India. Ultimately, I decided that I did not have the confidence to take the FLEX. I heard that the state of Florida had its own state board examination which was less grueling and detailed. If I passed it, I would be licensed to practice medicine there. I decided to chance it and took the exam in Tampa in 1977.

The exam was administered in a large hall where there were at least three hundred participants. It was multiple choice with a limited time to choose the best answer out of the five offered. There were many questions and it would be a race to answer all of them in the allotted time. We all needed to concentrate in a quiet environment to accomplish this task, but that day there were roofers on the building creating a racket. We complained to the monitors, but they said there was nothing they could do. A few minutes later, a candidate could not stand it any longer and started screaming at the monitors, saying "What the hell? I cannot continue with this awful racket above my head. For God's sake do something about it!" When I heard that scream, I was so shaken that my pencil flew out of my hand. After a discussion among themselves, the head monitor announced that they would give us an extra hour to finish the examination since they could not persuade the roofers to stop working. This decision seemed to satisfy us, and I completed my examination in time despite the noise. One fine morning in March of 1977 I got my results. I had passed my Florida state boards examination. I was so filled with joy that I started banging on the bathroom door, where Meena was taking a shower, shouting that I had passed. Finally, I was safe and secure in my career. I could stay in the States and practice psychiatry. I could feed my family.

In 1977, we found out that Suryakant, my sister's husband, was suffering from primary pulmonary hypertension. He traveled from their home in Dayton to the Mayo Clinic in Minnesota to see if there was a cure, but in vain. However, he was a courageous man who did not let this disease defeat his spirits. He continued to both work as an engineer and to pursue his business. He had been born and raised in Mumbai and had migrated to the US where he was employed as an engineer in Dayton. On a visit to India, he decided to get married. My father learned of Suryakant and arranged for my sister, then 19, to go out on a date with him. She was ambivalent about getting married to someone she hardly knew. But my father liked him, and thought him to be a hardworking, intelligent engineer. My father insisted and Anupama agreed to marry him within a few weeks. She had taken a big risk leaving her family and friends and flying thousands of miles away. To make it even more difficult, there were hardly any east Indians in Dayton. She worked as a legal secretary, but the salary was meager. So Suryakant decided to start a business of his own. He asked his brother, in India, to send semiprecious stones, small rocks and other small gift items to him. There was a market for this type of merchandise in the US. He taught Anupama to set up booths and sell the items during mall shows. Initially, she traveled within Ohio. Later, she started traveling to faraway places like New York City. She would stay overnight in a motel and rise early the next morning to drive to the local mall. She would carry many boxes of merchandise in and set up her booth. At the end of the day she would put the merchandise back in the boxes and head back to the motel. The next morning, she would travel to another city for another show. She worked hard and this was all new to her; traveling alone on American roads and staying in cities she had never heard of. Though tired and stressed at times, she kept on going. Eventually, she made some business contacts with wholesalers which would help them to expand the business.

I was busy with my residency and preparing for my examinations, but I made several trips to Dayton, to give emotional support to my sister and Suryakant. On one such visit, we decided to have a weekend outing in Burr Oak State Park, near Columbus. In addition to Anupama's family and mine, we were joined by our cousin and his family. During our stay, Suryakant had a seizure and was admitted to a private hospital in Columbus. I stayed with him, while Anupama went back to Dayton with her son. After a few days his condition improved enough for me to drive him home, only an hour's ride. On the way, he started breathing heavily and looked as if he was getting rapidly worse. I worried that he might lose consciousness and I sped up to reach a nearby hospital. After about half an hour I pulled up in front of a private hospital in Dayton and took him to the emergency room. From there he was transferred to the ICU. I was with him when he passed away on September 7, 1977. His funeral was well attended. My parents arrived from India a few days later to provide their emotional support for my grieving sister. It was a very sad and difficult time for all of us. But I managed to cope despite grief and the stress of residency and exams.

*   *   *

OSU always had a good football team and during my time in Columbus, my interest in football grew. I was lucky to see football hall of famer, Archie Griffin, play under the great coach, Woody Hayes. There was a long-standing football rivalry between the Ohio State Buckeyes and University of Michigan Wolverines. I attended one of these games at the OSU stadium with one of my colleagues. Though the Buckeyes played well, they narrowly lost to the Wolverines. Some of the Buckeye fans were not happy with this outcome, so they started creating chaos and damaging cars on a nearby street. My car happened to be parked there, but I managed to get it away before the mob got near me. The police got everything under control quickly. I also attended a similar game at the University of Michigan stadium with my cousin a few years later. The Buckeyes won that game and I celebrated with my cousin, though he was a Wolverines fan.

OSU also excelled in track and field events, producing outstanding sport figures such as Olympic gold medalist, Jesse Owens, and golf legend, Jack Nicklaus, who resides in Dublin, a suburb of Columbus.

As I began my OSU residency, we learned that Meena was pregnant with our second daughter. It was a difficult pregnancy. She threw up quite often and could not stand the smell of Indian food. She practically stopped cooking at home and since I neither had the time to cook nor did I know how to cook Indian food, we tried to manage with Mexican and pizza type restaurant food.

Meena gave birth to our second daughter in March at the OSU hospital. When we took her home, a pleasant nurse escorted us out and asked me what I was going to name her. I told her Paulomi, which seemed like a nice Indian name. But in the naming ceremony, a few days later, my sister, Anupama, renamed her Shilpi, saying that Paulomi was too difficult to pronounce. This was fine with me because in my culture the father's sister usually names the child. During the rare evening or weekend when I was not studying or on call, I spent valuable time with my family. My children were delightful, and I enjoyed taking them out to local playgrounds and parks. Meena was doing a great job of raising them while I was busy establishing my career.

I eventually bolstered up my courage and decided to take the FLEX examination after all. I wanted the option to practice medicine in any state. I decided to take the exam in Michigan. There, I was allowed to retake any section in which I might be unsuccessful in my first attempt. My evenings were generally taken up with preparations for the exam both at home and in the OSU library. It had been ten years since I had passed my medical school MBBS examination and my knowledge, in some subjects, had diminished considerably. So, after a hectic day of residency, I would pour over textbooks to refresh my medical knowledge. I had hardly any time to spend with my daughters. I was so exhausted with the stress of residency and preparing for FLEX that I was quite irritable on some days. I would inform Meena and the children to leave me alone and since Meena was also tired after her day of work and looking after our children, this led to some arguments. I felt guilty that I was remaining irritable and could not spend more quality time with my wife and children. But my main goal was to pass these difficult examinations, get a good job and provide for my family.

The first day of FLEX consisted of multiple-choice questions in anatomy, physiology, biochemistry, pathology, microbiology and pharmacology. The second day was multiple choice questions in the clinical sciences of medicine surgery, obstetrics and gynecology, preventive health, pediatrics and psychiatry. The final day consisted of assessing my clinical competence. A case history of a patient was presented, and I had to choose the right multiple-choice answer. Unsuccessful in my first attempt, I decided to take the examination again. As usual I was persistent and did not get discouraged. A few months later I made a second attempt and passed in June of 1978. The state of Ohio issued me a license to practice by reciprocity agreement with the state of Michigan. Now I could practice medicine in most of the United States.

CHAPTER 14

COLUMBUS, OHIO

Meena with Shefali and Shilpi in Columbus

I finished my psychiatry residency at OSU in July 1978 and obtained a job in a state-run facility. Meanwhile, I was preparing for my psychiatry board examination. Certification by the American Board of Psychiatry and Neurology was not mandatory, but it would raise my status among my peers and serve as a yardstick for measuring my knowledge and competence in psychiatry. Some employers, private and public, would hire only board-certified psychiatrists and in most cases, it meant higher pay. The examination consisted of two parts; one covering the theory of psychiatry and the other involved seeing two psychiatric patients whom I would interview, diagnose and recommend treatment. The examiners would then question me regarding my decisions. Additionally, they showed us actor-portrayed TV vignettes of patients with neurological problems then asked questions regarding those vignettes. This was a difficult examination, but I had the advantage of five years of recent psychiatry experience and training, in addition to countless lectures from our knowledgeable psychiatry teachers. Preparing for this examination, while not as difficult as the ECFMG and FLEX, still took away quality time from my family, whom I dearly loved. After a full day at work, I had to study in the evenings and on weekends. Meena did a great job of nurturing and taking care of the children and our stress levels, in general, were lower than before. I was making a decent salary for the first time and felt satisfied that I was providing for my family. We had bought a nice house in Worthington, a suburb of Columbus, and made friends whose company we enjoyed in our free time.

After months of preparation, I passed "part one written," the multiple choice portion of the examination, on my first attempt. Passing part two was another matter. I probably did not impress my examiners. I took it in two different cities and was unsuccessful both times. But the third time, in Kansas City in June 1981, was the charm. This certification was a feather in my cap and gave me more self-confidence. I always believed that candidates who are unsuccessful the first or second time, gather more knowledge and skills through continued preparation. Thus I became a more knowledgeable and a good psychiatrist. Though sometimes disheartened by my unsuccessful attempts at various examinations, I was persistent and I tried and tried again until I was successful.

I wanted to start my own private practice instead of working for the state. But I did not have the business acumen or the confidence. I knew it involved renting an office, buying furniture and office supplies, hiring office staff, advertising, and so on. In addition, there would be some initial expenditure which I could not afford. So, I started looking for a private practice psychiatrist who would be willing to take on a partner. But I was unsuccessful.

After an exhaustive search, it looked as though we might have to leave Columbus and find a job elsewhere. Leaving the beautiful city and our friends was not ideal. Meena loved city life because she had grown up in big cities and enjoyed the hustle and bustle. We liked our home, a new two story, nicely furnished house with a well-manicured lawn. I have many pleasant memories of riding bikes with my daughter, Shefali, in that neighborhood. But we did not have a choice.

Meena agreed that it would be better for the family if I found a job I liked, even if it was in a small town. The girls were young enough, ages 9 and 4, to move and make new friends. We could adjust just as we had done in Scotland and Wales. I was thankful to Meena for her understanding and support during this difficult time. So, I started applying for jobs all over the country through ads posted in such publications as the Psychiatric News. I was called for two or three interviews, including St Alban's Psychiatric Services in Beckley, West Virginia, a private psychiatric outpatient clinic run by a private psychiatric hospital.

It was a sad time for us. But I came across so many patients whose stressors were much worse than ours. They had experienced job loss, financial issues, relationship problems, loneliness, health issues, addiction, and many other life altering occurrences which made them depressed and anxious. Even though our circumstances were different, I empathized with these patients, knowing firsthand what it was like to feel that way. It probably made me a better psychiatrist. But more than that, their resilience and courage to deal with their issues helped me know that Meena and I would be able to face whatever life changes were about to happen.

With Shefali and Shilpi in Columbus

CHAPTER 15

BECKLEY, WEST VIRGINIA

At Grandview State Park Near Beckley

Meena and I traveled by car to Beckley, a five-hour trip from Columbus. The St Alban's mental health services clinic was located downtown in an old two-story house whose rooms had been converted into offices for clinical and clerical staff. This clinic was bought by a St Alban's Psychiatric Hospital in Virginia from another psychiatrist. It had originally been a private practice with an established patient load. I would serve as the medical director of this outpatient satellite psychiatric clinic and see outpatients for the purpose of referring them to St Alban's hospital if they needed inpatient care.

The staff consisted of a social worker, a psychologist and two secretaries. I had always wanted to do outpatient psychiatry in a private office where I would not have a boss on site. The administrator was impressed with my credentials, especially with me being board certified. They offered me the job with a decent salary and though I thought I would like the job; we were not very impressed with the area. Beckley is an old coal town of about fifty thousand people located among the beautiful hills of West Virginia, far from the big city life of Columbus which we had so enjoyed. We had decided that I would take the job for a couple of years until I could find a decent job in a more metropolitan area. One of the main reasons we also agreed to accept the job offer was because Meena's cousin and her husband, Rupa and Sunil, lived in nearby Charleston, WV. Being only an hour's drive from Beckley, it was nice to know that we had family live close by and once we settled, we did visit them and their son, Kabeer, often.

I relocated in April 1982, staying in a motel until July when my family would join me after Shefali had finished her school year. The clinic was nice enough to grant me Friday afternoons off so that I could drive to Columbus. I missed my family and friends in Ohio and made this trip every week for two months.

There were only a few Indian families in Beckley. We became friends with the couple, Chandrakant and Ila, who owned the small, old motel in downtown Beckley where I roomed. They were helpful and gave me some good advice and support during this time of change. They became our lifelong friends. Most of the Indian population were physicians and their families who had come from India and Africa.

Meanwhile, I was getting used to my new job. The clinic had added a female psychologist, well versed in cognitive behavioral therapy which had become popular. The social worker was an experienced counselor. I concentrated on initial psychiatric intakes, arriving at a diagnosis, laying out a treatment plan, and managing medications.

I had relied on tricyclic antidepressant medications in the past to treat very depressed patients. While they were efficacious, they had some uncomfortable side effects and some of them could be dangerous if a severely depressed patient decided to take a lethal overdose. Therefore, I had to be very careful in prescribing these medications. Newer antidepressants had come out which I felt were both efficacious and safer with fewer side effects. These targeted the serotonin receptors in the brain and were known as SSRIs (serotonin reuptake inhibitors). Later, a new generation of antidepressants came out which targeted the serotonin, norepinephrine or dopamine receptors. They boosted the levels of these neurotransmitters which resulted in the lifting of depression. Thus, I had more antidepressants in my armamentarium to treat patients with different types of depressive symptoms. Some SSRIs were also used to treat anxiety disorders. The pharmaceutical companies, psychiatrists and research scientists are targeting other neuroreceptors in the brain to come out with better and safer treatments for various types of psychiatric disorders and for the management of side effects. Now we are waiting for breakthroughs in the treatment and possible cure for Alzheimer's disease.

Alzheimer's is a form of dementia which usually affects people over 65 years of age. With approximately seventy-five million baby boomers (people born between 1946 and 1964) in the US, the number of potential

Alzheimer patients is staggering, especially if they live beyond eighty-five years of age. Since patients with severe Alzheimer's disease will most likely need full time institutional nursing care this will cause a severe strain on the health care budget, in addition to the inherent burden on caregivers. The Bill and Melinda Gates Foundation, whose primary focus has been infectious diseases, recently donated $50 million to find a cure for this dreadful disease.

Since the majority of my work involved psychopharmacology (the study of the effects of drugs on the mind and behavior), I started attending psychiatric conferences all over the US. This way, I remained current in the knowledge and the use of psychotropic medications for children, adults and geriatric patients; all of which I treated in the clinic.

My employers allowed me to "moonlight" on weekends to supplement my salary. I would do psychiatric evaluations on claimants who had applied for workers compensation; usually coal miners who had been injured on the job. Many had suffered back injuries due to rockfalls in the mines or lung damage from inhaling coal dust particles. Many had only a high school education and no other skills. Inability to work meant they could not support their families, and this led to stress, depression, and anxiety. The miners were often represented by their own attorneys who would have an orthopedic doctor evaluate the physical injury and have me do the permanent partial disability evaluation caused by the resulting psychological factors. A male psychologist would accompany me, traveling as far as Morgantown, Clarksburg, Pineville, and Logan. He would do the psychological testing and help me to come to a psychiatric diagnosis. I would interview the claimant and then assign the percentage of disability, according to the worker's compensation guidelines of the American Medical Association and submit my report to the attorney who would then pay me a fee. I was quite honest with my conclusions and did not always give a report that was favorable to the claimant. I would sometimes be called by the coal company's attorney to give a deposition in the presence of the claimant's attorney and a magistrate. Many times, the company's attorney would grill me in an aggressive manner regarding my evaluation and how I came to my conclusion. This was unnerving at times, but I took it in good stride. We also did social security disability evaluations. A claimant could receive benefits if he was found to be totally and permanently disabled, unable to perform substantial gainful employment for a total of twelve months usually due to a combination of his physical and psychological problems. The final decision was made by the Social Security Administration staff.

When traveling we would do evaluations in the hotel where we were staying. One memorable stay was at the Aracoma Hotel in Logan, named after a Native American princess. It was a four-story structure built in 1917. It had ninety-six rooms and at one time was one of the most prestigious hotels in West Virginia. Though it was renovated in the seventies, it was in somewhat shabby condition when we stayed there, but I enjoyed the old-style look and the nice lobby. This magnificent old hotel was destroyed in a fire in 2010 and subsequently demolished.

For the most part, the miners were simple, hard-working men performing manual labor underground, often six days a week to make enough money to support their families. The working conditions were difficult and potentially dangerous. They would spend about ten hours a day in the dark mine, lit by electric bulbs, often on a wet floor and under a low roof on their knees for hours at a time. The safety and conditions in the mines have improved somewhat over the years, but there are still explosions and accidents though rare, which result in the deaths of miners.

The coal mining industry is on the decline. Most of the coal was used for thermal power plants that have now switched to natural gas which is easy to burn and results in less pollution. This, of course, has led to layoffs causing financial hardship, depression and anxiety. This affects not only the miner, but also his wife who looks after the house and kids. I learned about the American protestant work ethic in West Virginia and tried to put that in practice in my own life. My staff and I did all that we could to treat these down-to-earth, friendly folks. Today, West Virginia has been affected by the opioid abuse epidemic, creating another challenge for the state and its people.

By 1996, the administrators of the St Alban's Clinic had decided to close it down though it was doing well. So, I decided to take a part time job in an out of state maximum security prison. This all male prison housed many prisoners, convicted of crimes ranging from murder to inflicting grievous injury to dealing drugs. Many inmates were high risk and violent offenders. The prison was secured by a razor wire security fence, electronic detection and a locking control system.

It is estimated that a high percent of state prisoners may have some type of psychiatric disorder. Many state hospitals for the chronically mentally ill had closed in the eighties and without access to outpatient psychiatric care, they became homeless and had to live without adequate psychiatric medications. When they broke the law, they would end up imprisoned because the seriously mentally ill (SMI) are more likely to be incarcerated than hospitalized. I felt that my skills were needed but I was not sure whether I could handle the stress of dealing with the prison population while I was worried about my safety. I strove to rid myself of these negative thoughts and decided to rise to the challenge with courage. I remembered a saying by Eleanor Roosevelt "You gain strength, courage and confidence by every experience in which you really stop to look fear in the face… You must do the thing you think you cannot do."

Each time the prison door closed behind me; I also became a prisoner for a few hours. All the prisoners were required to follow the rules and guards were to be respected. I was given an alarm which was attached to my belt. In case of danger, I could pull a knob and an alarm would go off. Hopefully a security guard would come running and reach me in about five minutes. Breaking the rules was met with punishment, sometimes severe. We were given training in how to calm down an agitated patient with verbal skills.

This prison had a good reputation of treating the prisoners well. It provided a variety of services to the prisoners. The prison had a post office, library, mechanics workshop, vocational school, gymnasium, medical clinic and a chapel. It had a psychiatric unit where inmates with SMI (schizophrenia, bipolar disorder, PTSD, substance abuse, depression, anxiety and personality disorders) were housed, each had a cell of their own. Many of these prisoners responded to antipsychotics, mood stabilizers, or antidepressants and became much less agitated and violent. They also benefited from cognitive behavior therapy, relaxation, supportive and group therapy. Some of the men had committed their crimes under the influence of street drugs and alcohol, and therefore behaved rationally in the prison because they were not under the influence. I avoided giving stimulants, benzodiazepines or opioids to prisoners because they would either abuse them, or trade them with other prisoners. The nurses dispensed most of the medications in a crushed form to preclude their diverting it to other prisoners. All the prisoners had to take medications under the direct observation of the nurses. Prisoners were not allowed to keep medication on their person or in their cells. Many depressed prisoners were placed on antidepressants and referred to counselors for psychotherapy. Many of them responded to treatment. Some of them started attending church services and found strength through spirituality.

One such prisoner occupied a cell in the psychiatric unit. He had a traumatic childhood, as did many prisoners. He was born in the inner city and was given up for adoption at a young age. He was shuttled from one foster family to another where some of the foster parents allegedly abused him, both physically and emotionally. His story was a typical one. He started rebelling and getting into fights in school. He got into drugs at a young age, starting with marijuana and progressing to meth and opioids. He dropped out of school and joined an inner-city gang where he graduated to selling street drugs. He was happy to make a lot of money, but there was a price to pay. He was often involved in fights with rival gang members over control of the drug traffic. He was jailed twice for disorderly conduct, carrying controlled substances and causing injury. Both times he managed to get out after spending a few months in local jails. The police were waiting for a chance to put him away for a long time since they were aware that he was a drug dealer. Eventually he tried to sell heroin to an undercover agent and was sentenced to thirty years in prison. He was transferred to our prison after getting into fights in the previous prison. In our prison he became a member of a notorious gang and soon garnered a reputation for violence. He was involved in a knife fight and in a second incident, he threatened a prison guard. He was punished by being placed in solitary confinement, which was a small cell with a bed, a toilet, and a small window with a view of the sky. After two weeks in solitary confinement he became frustrated, agitated, depressed and had suicidal thoughts. He was transferred to the locked psychiatric unit. When I saw him, I was not sure whether he was really depressed or whether it was a ploy to get him out of solitary confinement. Our psychologist performed objective psychological testing on him and felt that he was depressed. I placed him on an antidepressant and referred him for counseling with the psychologist. After a few weeks, he was feeling better and no longer felt suicidal. Placing him in solitary confinement had taught him a lesson. He enrolled in vocational rehabilitation training and worked out in the gym for a few hours a day, which tended to calm his frustration and reduce his anger. He knew that if he behaved well, he had a better chance of parole. I discharged him from the psychiatric unit and transferred him to the general population where he adjusted and functioned as a model prisoner.

After working for a few months in prison, I quit to start my own private psychiatric practice. I felt happy that I had diagnosed and adequately treated quite a few prisoners with interesting psychiatric problems. The unit was certainly calmer when I left. This had been an unusual and memorable experience in my life that proved I could overcome my anxiety and perform under difficult circumstances. It was a real boost to my self-confidence.

In the meanwhile, my children were growing up in a house that we bought in Maxwell Hill, a suburb of Beckley. Though modest in size, it looked stately with its white brick and long columns. There were tall trees scattered through the yard and our patio was surrounded by blooming rhododendron bushes, the state flower of West Virginia. There were kids always around as my daughters made many friends in the neighborhood. Nearby, Shefali and Shilpi often visited Shirley, a previous coworker of mine, with whom we became very close. The girls adored her and they often would run away to her house to indulge in some of her southern cooking or complain to her about Meena and me, particularly when they would get in trouble. We appreciated that they had someone like Shirley who understood their "Americanized" wishes for more independence, but yet ensured that they respected our more strict Indian ways of raising them. Living in that house in Beckley, our family formed many lifelong friendships and cherished memories. We realized what a blessing in disguise it was to have landed a job in small town, Beckley, WV, after all.

In front of Our Home in Beckley, WV

**Former Psychiatric Team Member and Close
Family Friend, Shirley, With My Daughters**

CHAPTER 16

PSYCHOTHERAPY APPROACHES

In the course of my studies, I came across the teachings of psychiatrists and psychologists who specialized in psychoanalysis at the turn of the century, such as Sigmund Freud, Carl Jung, Erik Erikson and Alfred Adler. I was particularly impressed by the writings of Erik Erikson, the American psychologist who said that a child's growth, psychological development and identity was nurtured in their environment. These teachings, combined with those of Ellis, Beck and the great scriptures of the world deepened my understanding of my own personality makeup and aided my self-growth; thus, enhancing my patient care.

In the 1950s, psychologist and therapist, Albert Ellis, developed Rational Emotive Behavior Therapy (REBT). According to him, a person's irrational and dysfunctional thoughts and beliefs result in self-defeating behavior. Therefore, the therapy focused on replacing irrational thoughts with rational thoughts.

Psychiatrist, Aaron Beck, is considered the father of cognitive behavior therapy (CBT). Developed in the 60s, CBT is based on the theory that thought distortion and maladaptive behaviors play a role in the development and maintenance of psychiatric disorders. The resulting symptoms and level of distress can be reduced by correcting cognitive distortions and learning better ways of coping. CBT is the most widely used evidence-based practice for improving mental health. Dr. Beck, along with his daughter Dr. Judith Beck, have trained thousands of professionals worldwide in the use of CBT. One of Beck's students, David Burns, MD, wrote "Feeling Good," a book that had a big influence on me. It not only helped me with counseling my patients, but also with my own distress caused by my occasional negative thoughts.

According to the cognitive model, anxiety and depression always result from distorted negative thoughts. Some of the self-defeating beliefs that trigger sadness or anxiety in physicians are the self pressure to become perfect in our profession, to feel approved by everybody, and achieve as much as possible. For instance, in my earlier years, if I was unsuccessful in passing an examination on the first attempt, I would get down on myself believing that I was not intelligent enough to become a physician. This would lead to the conclusion that I had also failed as a husband, parent and a son. But after reading "Feeling Good" and recognizing some of my own cognitive distortions, I began to challenge and change my way of thinking. I realized that I could pass on the second or third attempt, acquiring additional knowledge and as a result become a better practitioner. Passing the examination on the first attempt had nothing to do with my success or failure in my personal life. That required other skills which I was trying to improve upon. In this way, I started feeling better about myself.

Newer psychotherapies that have emerged involve mindfulness training. This is the ability to be aware of the present moment, while calmly acknowledging and accepting one's feelings, thoughts and bodily sensations. This is achieved by focusing on either breath, body, senses or your thoughts; usually done through the regular practice of meditation techniques, thus making the person feel more peaceful and happy. These therapies have been found to be effective and are being widely used.

There are several other psychotherapy techniques developed over the years allowing a therapist to choose the appropriate approach based on their expertise and the patient's symptomatology and needs. A variety of these psychotherapy techniques were utilized within the various settings I worked. I was blessed to have worked with competent and experienced counselors, social workers and psychologists who were able to implement these theories effectively with our patients. Their moods and relationships improved and they were able to function better in their occupational, social and personal lives. It was gratifying to see them function better in society.

CHAPTER 17

PRIVATE PRACTICE

Staff of Sunrise Psychiatric Services in Beckley, West
Virginia, Picture Courtesy of The Register-Herald

In 1997, with the encouragement of my wife, I started my own private psychiatric clinic, Sunrise Psychiatric Services. The clinical staff consisted of a child psychologist and a social worker who specialized in counseling children between the ages of four and eighteen, a social worker who did play therapy with children and Christian counseling with adults, and a second psychologist with whom I had worked earlier, who specialized in CBT and psychological evaluations for adults. Meena was the office manager. Since I had not specialized in medication management for children, I took some special courses and became certified in adolescent psychiatry.

Children and their parents were initially interviewed by our child psychologist. Sometimes, she would also talk to the teacher, school psychologist or a caseworker, if necessary, to get the whole history. She would do a thorough intake, including psychological testing, come to a diagnosis and suggest treatment. This would consist of either counseling by our social workers or with her and a possible referral to me for medication management. Depending on the needs of the child, the counseling could include both the child and the parents.

We had an eleven-year-old male patient, whose parents brought him to the clinic at the suggestion of his teachers. They complained that he was not paying attention, was hyperactive and constantly fidgeted or moved about. He would talk excessively and out of turn, and in general was disruptive; acting like the class clown. He would not finish his school assignments and his grades were suffering as a result. His parents stated that this behavior was also evident at home. I made a tentative diagnosis of attention deficit hyperactivity disorder (ADHD) and referred him to our child psychologist who performed psychological testing and interviewed the parents. She confirmed the diagnosis of ADHD and she began counseling the child. She tried behavior therapy and helped him organize his tasks and complete his schoolwork on time. She helped him monitor his own conduct and taught him to praise himself for thinking before acting. She advised his parents to apply these practices at home and to establish clear rules with consistent consequences for breaking them. Since he was not progressing fast enough with psychotherapy the psychologist referred him to me for medication management which the parents were in favor of. I prescribed a stimulant, and informed the parents about the potential side effects, drug interactions, risks and benefits. They understood and consented to treatment. Stimulants act on brain receptors regulating dopamine and norepinephrine. The patient started showing improvement within a few days with no side effects and tolerance of the medication. The teachers said that he had calmed down, was not disruptive and was paying attention in class. Both the parents and teachers were happy with the improvement in his behavior. He was completing his school assignments, played with other kids in the neighborhood without getting into fights and his grades started improving. The prognosis was that we might be able to discontinue his stimulant after a year. After seeing many depressed patients sometimes it was a relief to see hyperactive kids running around in the clinic laughing and carrying on.

A sixteen-year-old girl was brought in by her mother because she seemed depressed. In my initial interview with her, she stated that she was feeling sad, had little interest in her activities, had become withdrawn, and was suffering from insomnia. She felt socially awkward and had stopped visiting many of her friends. She had even stopped playing basketball, a sport she was fond of. Her grades were suffering, and she felt hopeless and anxious. Her mother thought that her boyfriend breaking up with her might be a contributing factor. Adolescents live in a small world consisting of school and home. Any problems in these settings can trigger psychological problems. Interpersonal conflicts, stress and substance abuse can trigger depression and possible suicidal thoughts. Her parents had divorced two years before which bothered her. She missed her dad, seeing him only once a month. I learned that he had suffered from major depression a few years before and had responded to antidepressants and psychiatric treatment. She denied having any suicidal ideation and had no prior history of suicidal attempts. I diagnosed her as having major depression. After psychological testing and evaluation by our child psychologist, it was confirmed that she suffered from major depression, a single episode. We decided to treat her with a combination of SSRI medication plus cognitive behavior and interpersonal therapy to be performed by our social worker. The risks and benefits of treatment were explained to the mother, which she understood and consented to treatment. I informed the mother to watch her closely for a few weeks for any emergence of suicidal ideation and to call us, if necessary. The presence of suicidal ideation in teenagers was taken very seriously in our clinic since teenagers are more apt to follow through. Her weekly therapy included bolstering her self-worth and development of social skills. Along with her medication this brought about significant improvement. She became less depressed, resumed playing sports, improved her grades, and began socializing again. Her parents helped her by resolving whatever small differences they had and agreeing that her father would see her more often. It was always gratifying to see our patients improve with a combination of medications and psychotherapy.

Meena was invaluable as the office manager. She supervised three administrative staff members who were responsible for the managerial and financial aspects of the clinic's daily operation. She would often stay late until 11pm to complete her tasks including billing Medicaid and the insurance companies for services rendered in the clinic. I used to worry about her working all alone in the dark. It was not easy to manage a private psychiatric clinic like ours due to the large number of staff involved and difficulty in meeting the overhead. Medicaid payments were minimal. But we managed. We were blessed with dedicated clinical and administrative staff who provided excellent service. We worked well as a team. On our annual visit to Beckley from Florida, the Sunrise Psychiatric Services alumni make it a point to meet, have lunch and reminisce about the happy times we had working together.

Singing Christmas Carols During Our Staff Christmas Party

CHAPTER 18

SHEFALI

Shefali's Graduation Picture from West Virginia University

Meanwhile, on the home front, our daughters were growing up and enjoying school life in Beckley. Shefali was a tomboy and enjoyed playing sports with the girls and boys in the neighborhood. She was a talented basketball player and had served as a team captain in junior high. She was also successful at track and would often come in first in the 400-meter and 4X400m relay races. It was a delight to see her competing in these track and field competitions.

It was important to me to share some of our East Indian values with Shefali. So, when she became a teenager, I took her on a spiritual retreat to a Siddha Yoga ashram located in the Catskill Mountains of upstate New York. This ashram was headed by a young female spiritual leader. The daily schedule consisted of morning meditation sessions, followed by seminars on Indian scriptures. In the evening, we sang spiritual hymns accompanied by Indian instrumental music. Shefali initially resisted going with me to the ashram because of her preconceived stereotypes and notions of what a place like this is. However, once there, she seemed to really enjoy the beauty and calm of the environment. She became even more open-minded about it when she realized that so many of the other youth that were there were non-Indians, and still chose to embrace these Indian philosophies. Hopefully, Shefali benefited from this experience and learned the value of meditation and treating others with love and compassion. I know I did.

In the ashram, everybody was treated as an equal and we adults were asked to perform seva (a selfless service) within its community. My assigned task was to perform seva by serving tea to others in the cafeteria. It occurred to me that I had never been expected to serve anyone before. This was a humbling thought as I reflected on why that was, especially when I realized that the individual doing seva next to me did work in the service industry, serving tea. Who knows, he too, may have been surprised to learn that I was a doctor! At the ashram, the idea was to learn to interact with others without stereotypes and attachments to our labels, status and privilege, and to carry this into our daily life. In this way you become more free to relate to the soul of another, a more compassionate way to be. The experiences there have not left me and have served as a reminder to be humble and polite in my dealings with different types of people.

Back at home, Shefali had the usual teenage moods and disagreements with us. I am sure she thought that we were too strict. She was not allowed to stay out late or spend the night at other friends' houses. We allowed her to go out in a group with boys and girls, but not on individual dates. These were some of the generational and cultural differences between raising children here and in India. We were okay with Shefali not necessarily having an arranged marriage, but we did not feel it was appropriate for her to date too early in life. This would be a distraction from her studies and felt that engaging in these activities would ruin her reputation in our community. Despite our strict rules on what she was allowed to do and with whom, Shefali was popular in school and was nominated to the Homecoming Court in junior high and Prom Court in high school. When she graduated from Woodrow Wilson High School in 1991, we threw a graduation party for her. Our close friends were invited and my parents also visited from India to attend the event. They were very proud of her and my father gave a speech which was well-received.

Shefali applied to many colleges, but we decided to send her to West Virginia University in Morgantown for her undergraduate degree. We had heard that it had a reputation for being a party school, but students could get a good education. Plus, we liked that she would be no more than three hours away from home. Like many of the Indian students who were children of physicians and other professionals, she pursued Biology as her major, hoping to then go to medical school. However, Shefali did not do well in her biology classes and started getting subpar grades. We were not sure whether this was due to her dislike of the curriculum or for some other reason, such as partying. We would receive letters from the dean informing us that she would be removed from school unless she improved her grades, whereupon we would make the three hour road trip to Morgantown to show our concern and give advice. To our relief, she started taking her academics more seriously. In her junior year she changed her major to psychology and seemed to find her niche and her grades improved substantially after that.

Meena and I had given her a Toyota Camry to drive around and to easily make her visits back home to Beckley from college. But it seemed, each time she made a trip she would get a speeding ticket, and each time she would try to get out of paying the fine by giving some excuse to the court. I had no choice but to take the car away from her for a while. She reacted by saying, "I am in college and you are grounding me!!" It was difficult for us to be strict with our grown-up children, but we felt we were guiding them in the right direction by setting limits.

Shefali met a handsome boy, Pranav, at a wedding in Columbus, Ohio. He had just graduated from The Ohio State University College of Dentistry, and it so happened, he had gained admission to WVU to complete his three-year orthodontic specialty the same year Shefali graduated from there. On one of their first outings together, the summer after Shefali's graduation and when Pranav was beginning his orthodontic program, Shefali decided to go whitewater rafting with him and his new classmates down the New River, which was near our home in Beckley. While maneuvering one of the most difficult rapids, Shefali and Pranav both fell into the fast moving water, and the current pulled Shefali under the raft. Luckily, she found her way out from under it and Pranav managed to somehow get back into the raft. With quick thinking, before she could get sucked back under, he bent over and yanked her out of the water and into the raft to safety. This was like Tarzan rescuing Jane! Their love for each other blossomed after that. They laugh about it now saying they were traumatically bonded for life.

Soon after, Shefali invited him home to meet Meena and me. We were impressed with his intelligence and bubbly personality. On her way out with him, Shefali asked, "Dad, what do you think of him?" I gave her a thumbs up and Meena nodded in agreement. We were all happy.

At summer's end, we moved Shefali to Chicago, Illinois. She was accepted to the Illinois School of Professional Psychology Chicago Campus to begin her post-graduate career. We found her a fancy apartment in a tall building near the posh Michigan Avenue in downtown Chicago. Though it was hard on our wallet, we enjoyed our days visiting Chicago, eating in high-end restaurants and window shopping. This was our first experience living in a mega American city. Shefali and Pranav continued their long distance relationship while studying in different states. About a year into their relationship, talks of marriage began and Pranav proposed to Shefali at the top of the Navy Pier ferris wheel overlooking the Chicago skyline. Shefali, who was scared of heights, was elated and happily accepted, and then demanded to be quickly brought back down to the ground. Because both Pranav and Shefali were still studying, Shefali asked Meena if she would plan the wedding for her. The decision was to have the wedding in India because Pranav's parents lived there, even though that meant most of their friends from America would not be able to attend.

The wedding festivities were to begin in December of 1996. Pranav's parents asked if they could host the couple's formal engagement ceremony in Baroda, where they reside. His father, Vinod Patel, was the retired Dean of Fine Arts at the prestigious Maharaja Sayajirao University of Baroda. He had many friends, relatives and colleagues whom he wished to invite to the ceremony. Meena and I decided to have the wedding a week after the engagement on January 2, 1997 at a beautiful hotel along the beach in Mumbai. Meena's sister and her husband, Joytsna and Asheet, and her Uncle Sharad, helped us with the elaborate arrangements. My father, who lived and worked in South

India, was very excited to have the wedding in India and also invited a lot of his friends and relatives to the wedding.

A few days before the engagement ceremony, Shefali traveled to Baroda to meet her in-laws for the first time. She was nervous, but they welcomed her warmly with a houseful of guests that Pranav had known since his childhood. Shefali had to get used to the Indian culture, customs and environment. India had changed since I left it in 1973. Prosperity was evident in big cities, like Mumbai, due to the high-tech and economic boom. Skyscrapers were rising all over the city and the rich were getting richer. About 300 million middle-class Indians had become more prosperous. Many of them were able to afford cars or two-wheelers, but the basic infrastructure and roads had not kept up with the increase in traffic and the roads became very congested. It took a long time to go from one place to another. The city is trying to remedy this by building new roads and an underground Metro Railway. Bribery and corruption remained rampant and many Indians still impoverished. India had become a land of contrasts. The rich lived in lavish apartments with servants to take care of their every need. Many of the servants, chauffeurs, and factory workers have flocked to the city from rural areas in search of opportunities. They cannot afford to live in expensive apartments, so many live in shacks. Some are surprisingly well-furnished! Some servants are fortunate and live in the same apartment as their employers and are treated well. When I visited India in 2020, I noticed that many of the slums where the poor live were gradually being eradicated and they were being displaced to low-cost housing apartments.

Often there is culture shock when seeing the overcrowded cities with heavy traffic and pollution, as well as the sadness of seeing the poverty stricken areas. But, with the very short time we had there, we did our best to focus on the happiness of the celebrations to come. The engagement party kicked off the beginning of the festivities. Upon our family's arrival to Baroda, Pranav's parents had made excellent arrangements for our stay and the formal engagement ceremony went off well. It was a double engagement ceremony as Pranav's older brother was also getting engaged. Almost 1000 people attended the event, including the Prince of Baroda! The ceremony was performed by a priest followed by a feast for all of the guests. His father's former students had prepared an elaborate artistic display of fruits and vegetables carved into mini figurines. It was a sight to see!

The next day, we headed to Mumbai for the wedding. The wedding parties were housed in several different hotels and Shefali was getting excited to see what her mother had planned for the wedding, as she had left it all up to her. Indian weddings are often made up of many events that carry different religious or cultural significance, and Meena, with the help of her sister, did a wonderful job organizing the events. The night before the wedding, one of the events we celebrated was garba, which is our traditional Gujarati style of dancing where we dance in large circles as a group. We also thoroughly enjoyed doing raas, where men and women dance with sticks in their hand synchronizing their choreography with the beat of Indian drums. For this party, we catered and served delicious foods and alcohol, and Meena had hired an upbeat live band that kept us dancing under the stars late into the night.

The next day the wedding was to take place in a big hall in a hotel facing Juhu Beach. As was the tradition, the bridegroom's wedding party, the baraat, came dancing down the road with a band blaring popular Bollywood music. Pranav was seated on a horse dressed in traditional princely attire with a turban on his head and a sword in his hand. A passing bus carrying Japanese tourists was so enthralled with the site that they blocked the party and started taking videos and photographs! After a few minutes they let the party proceed on to the wedding venue. Our bridal party welcomed them at the entrance of the hotel. Shefali greeted Pranav by putting a garland around his neck. She looked beautiful in her traditional Indian wedding saree, which were the colors of white, red, and gold. Pranav and Shefali took their vows around the sacred fire, in front of a priest who was chanting Hindu and Jain slokas (prayer verses). This was followed by a delicious lunch and reception that faced the oceanside. The gentlemen were dressed in suits and the women looked beautiful in their colorful sarees and jewelry. My father was very distinguished in his Nehru suit. My parents were happy that we had decided to do Shefali's wedding in India. They thoroughly enjoyed being with their children and grandchildren. We were also delighted to have my sister and her son, Anupama and Anand, my other sister and her husband, Shobhana and Chandrasen, and their sons, Prashant and Jesal, as well as my brother, Mukesh, attend the wedding. Meena's parents, sister and brother-in-law, Jyotsna and Asheet, along with their daughter and son, Kanisha and Kuntal, also attended the wedding. It was a good bonding time for the entire extended family. Pranav, his parents, Vinod and Gopa, his brother and new wife, Nilay and Vaishali, and their extended family and friends thoroughly enjoyed the celebration.

After the wedding, feeling very down to leave India and to leave one another, Shefali and Pranav had to go back to their separate universities and resume their studies. Shefali received her Master's Degree in psychology six months later in 1997. Following her Master's program, Shefali deferred her acceptance into the doctoral program for a year because she missed Pranav. She moved back to her alma mater, WVU, for a year while her husband finished his final third year of orthodontic residency. Once completed, they moved back to Chicago and Pranav began his orthodontic career and Shefali started her Doctor of Psychology program back at the Illinois School of Professional Psychology. Living on a tight budget, they rented a studio apartment, and between working and studying, they enjoyed the Chicago city life as much as they could afford.

Shefali's Clinical Psychology program kept her extremely busy. I was impressed by her ability to keep up with the demands of a doctoral program while also adjusting to her new married life. This included living jointly with her in-laws who would visit from India and stay for months at a time. Needless to say, it was cozy living conditions! But, Shefali loved her in-laws and did not find it to be a negative experience. In 2000, Pranav and Shefali moved to the western suburbs of Chicago close to where Pranav decided to open his first orthodontic practice.

While he was busy building his practice, Shefali began her clinical internship year at an outpatient community centered Health and Human Services Department (HHS) in a northwest suburb that required her to commute close to an hour each way. During her internship she continued to gain competence in providing psychotherapy to individuals, couples, and families of diverse backgrounds. With supervisions, she helped her clients work through issues such as depression, anxiety, school and work problems, and relationship difficulties. In addition, she conducted assessments and therapy for municipal employees, such as police and firefighters, and offered prevention-focused seminars to the community on topics such as parenting.

By this time in her training, Shefali had also worked with a number of clients on sensitive issues particularly pertaining to trauma, abuse and domestic violence. During her post-graduate years, I was proud of her involvement with a domestic violence agency, Apna Ghar (translates to "Our Home"), that works not only with, but largely, the underserved South Asian immigrant population. She volunteered on this organization's Junior Board, composed of young adult men and women, including Pranav, to help raise awareness on issues related to gender violence to the younger generation. One year, she even gave the main speech during their annual fundraising event, where the money raised helps Apna Ghar provide services like legal advocacy, counseling, and emergency shelter and housing to survivors and their families.

Soon after moving to the suburbs and moving into their new home, Shefali became pregnant with my first granddaughter, Raya. Meena and I were overjoyed, but also worried for Shefali. On top of her rigorous training requirements, Shefali had a difficult pregnancy. But, she was fortunate that she had an accommodating internship environment that also allowed her to work part-time post-delivery. When working, Pranav and Shefali decided to place Raya in a private home daycare setting so that she would be in a loving warm environment while they were away at work.

We were all very proud of Shefali when she graduated from her doctoral program. She had grown up to be a beautiful, intelligent young woman with a good head on her shoulders. Meena's parents, Shivlal and Sunanda, and her sister and brother-in-law, Jyotsna and Asheet, even came from India to see her receive her well earned Psy.D. diploma. The keynote speaker at her graduation was Dr. Patch Adams, an American trained physician, whose life has been depicted in a motion picture starring Robin Williams. He opened the Gesundheit Institute in rural West Virginia and practiced social medicine. He used humor with his patients, and his colleagues and he did not charge fees to patients or bill third-party insurance. To my knowledge, he covers his fees through donations and speaking engagements around the world. He talked to Shefali's graduating class about the value and importance of counseling mental health patients, instead of just prescribing them psychotropic medication. He also encouraged them to serve humanity and not charge fees to poor patients. This was an enlightening speech that made me reflect on my own practice. I had a practice where half of my patients were on Medicaid, which paid minimally for our services. Yet, we were still happy to treat these underserved folks. His speech reinforced and validated the work my staff and I did with our patients. Watching her graduate and become a doctor, I could not be happier that Shefali had chosen a profession where her work would directly impact patient lives in profound ways. I guess all the years of Shefali hearing my psycho-babble sunk in and fueled her interest in psychology and desire to help others. Truly, in this case, the apple didn't fall too far from the tree!

Following her graduation, Shefali chose to continue on in a post-doctoral capacity at HHS because of its positive work environment and her need to acquire enough supervised clinical hours to take her licensing exam. While she was busy balancing her work, studying for the licensing exam, and raising Raya, Shefali's in-laws decided to move from India to be close to their first grandchild. Around Raya's second birthday they arrived and split their time living between Shefali's house and her brother-in-law's home in California. Though they did not have a driver's license initially, and there was a slight language barrier in communicating, both Shefali and her in-laws adjusted well to living with one another. Shefali was glad to have their company and help in raising Raya. And, soon she was pregnant again with my second granddaughter, Ayana.

When Shefali finished her postdoctoral training and finally became a licensed psychologist, to her surprise, she was offered a permanent job as an Assistant Director at the Health and Human Services. She gratefully accepted the job. In her new capacity, she was given more responsibility in attending to policy issues, health and wellness services provided by the nurses to the community, and supervision and training of doctoral level interns. Sometimes, Shefali's days were long due to late therapy sessions often ending at 9pm and then her hour commute home. She missed seeing the girls on nights like these. With both Shefali and Pranav working, managing the house, kids, and spending quality time with her inlaws, life was becoming more challenging. Pranav's orthodontic practice was growing and they were becoming financially more stable. After a lot of thought, Shefali decided to submit her resignation so that she could be more present for the family as a whole and find more balance. Despite all the hard work she put into becoming a psychologist, Shefali realized she wanted to have the same presence in her daughter's lives as Meena had in hers and Shilpi's lives. She felt that she could always choose to go to work later, and in the meantime, use her psychological understanding to help her in raising her children. I admire the sacrifice she has made and know that it will be one that she will never regret.

**Shefali and Pranav's Wedding
with Both Sets of Parents in Mumbai**

CHAPTER 19

VETERANS ADMINISTRATION HOSPITAL

At VA Medical Center

When we first opened the clinic, I did not have enough patients to keep me busy, so I took a part time job two days a week as an outpatient psychiatrist at the Veterans Administration (VA) hospital. The hospital was medium sized with inpatient medical, surgical beds, an emergency room, a large outpatient department, and specialty clinics. The staff consisted of two psychiatrists, two physician assistants, two social workers and a couple of nurses. In 2007, when I joined them full time, the clinical staff had grown to about forty. Veterans from Operation Enduring Freedom (OEF) in Afghanistan and Operation Iraqi Freedom (OIF) were returning home with psychiatric problems and Congress had allotted large sums of money to the VA to treat them. Many were suffering from post-traumatic stress disorder (PTSD) from both of these operations, as well as from the Vietnam War Era (1961 to 1995). According to the US archives, 58,000 Americans were killed and over 150,000 were wounded in Vietnam. It is estimated that more than one million Vietnamese civilians and military personnel had been killed during the same period. While many American recruits were drafted, 75 percent of our forces volunteered. It was amazing to me that so many patriotic Americans readily went to Vietnam to fight for their motherland. Many of them answered the call of duty without fully understanding why the war was fought or the politics involved.

This is the story of one such Vietnam veteran. Treyton was drafted in 1968 when he was 18 and still in high school. His parents were afraid that he might be seriously injured or killed while in battle. Treyton had to choose between going to Vietnam, being jailed, or fleeing the country and being branded a coward for the rest of his life. The war had become increasingly unpopular at home and there were many protests. He decided to go, and he hoped that he would return home safe. After six months of jungle warfare training stateside, a military transport took him to Vietnam. He formed a close bond with his fellow platoon members in a remote area of South Vietnam and considered them as his brothers. Often while on patrol it rained for days at a time and he had to wade through rice paddies and jungle undergrowth infested with insects. The Viet Cong would sleep during the day in underground tunnels and come out at night to attack when they felt the Americans would be more vulnerable. One night, while serving as sentry, Treyton heard a noise as if an animal was passing nearby. He woke up his buddies who picked up their guns, just in case. When he fired a shot in the direction of the noise, hoping to scare the animal away, to his surprise there was a return fire. They took cover and a firefight ensued during which a member of his unit was shot in the leg. Bleeding and crying in pain, the soldier was given a morphine shot by a medic. Treyton was very frightened that he might die. They radioed for help and a helicopter arrived about a half an hour later and started firing in the area where the enemy was thought to be. He heard a few screams and then the noise stopped. The helicopter landed nearby, and the wounded soldier was taken to the nearest base for treatment. Treyton's platoon was soon replenished with new soldiers and they were told to continue their patrolling duties.

After this experience, Treyton remained anxious and started having nightmares. Despite this he had to continue performing his duties. Like many of his comrades, he started drinking and using marijuana just so that he could sleep. He was involved in a few more firefights where his left hand was injured and he witnessed one of his buddies die, a traumatic life event for him. While being treated at a nearby base hospital, he was diagnosed as having severe anxiety with PTSD symptoms. From there, he was flown to Japan where they operated on his hand and eventually found him to be unfit for duty. He received an honorable discharge and was sent home. Expecting a hero's welcome, he instead was greeted with negativity by antiwar demonstrators and was being referred to as a baby killer. This made him angrier and more depressed. He stopped informing people that he was a Vietnam veteran. His family and friends noticed that he had become aloof and he angered easily. He stopped socializing and started drinking more, adding to his depression and anxiety. He had insomnia and nightmares and woke up in sweats at night thinking that he was in a firefight in Vietnam. The sound of a plane or a helicopter flying above his house would make him nervous and he would dive for cover.

At the VA hospital he was detoxed from alcohol and placed on antidepressants and Prazosin, which helped his depression, PTSD and insomnia. He also received intensive counseling including cognitive behavior therapy, eye movement desensitization and reprocessing therapy, substance abuse counseling and group therapy. After a few months of outpatient psychiatric treatment, his counselor suggested that he take up a job to occupy his mind. He decided to work in the mines, a tough job that kept him occupied six days a week and left him little time to think of Vietnam. During this time, he met a woman who was understanding and supportive. On one of his clinical visits, he brought in his Purple Heart that he had received for his courageous service. I thanked him for his service, and he was appreciative of the fact that the United States government and several people were grateful and acknowledged his service.

* * *

The course of history was to change after the September 11 terrorist attacks on the World Trade Center and the Pentagon. By March 2003, Operation Iraqi Freedom (OIF) was launched and by April, a sectarian civil war and insurgency took over. Our all-volunteer military forces were not welcome in this area and came under constant mortar, rocket and sniper fire. Around 4500 American troops lost their lives and thousands more were injured. More than fifteen percent of OIF veterans suffered from PTSD, depression and/or substance abuse.

The Afghanistan war (Operation Enduring Freedom) or OEF started in October of 2001. Recently a peace deal has been signed and the United States may withdraw its troops in 14 months. About 2400 American troops have been killed. Quite a few of the returning veterans also suffered from mental health problems. These veterans came home to a large variety of services available for good psychiatric treatment and, unlike the Vietnam veterans, they were given a warm welcome by the American public.

At the VA, we would hear many stories of veterans who suffered psychological trauma from their wartime experiences. Osvaldo's story presented here illustrates some common themes that many vets share. He was an Iraq War (OIF) veteran who enlisted in 2000. He settled down to routine army life, living on a military base with his wife and two year old son, whom he adored. He had received training to fight a traditional land-based war as an infantry soldier. His life changed dramatically when the OIF was launched and he was deployed to fight the war. Luckily, the weather was still cool in March when his unit was ordered to march towards Baghdad in their heavy uniforms and full gear. He had been preparing for this invasion for many days, and he was anxious to get it done with. Not knowing what type of enemy-fire they would encounter, Osvaldo proceeded with a mixture of courage and anxiety. Although they encountered some mortar fire, they were able to move forward with little resistance. Following a decisive victory in April, he thought that peace would prevail in Iraq, but chaos ensued. The troops were assigned to patrol the dangerous streets of Baghdad to maintain law and order in very hot summer temperatures and desert conditions. When one of his buddies was injured by sniper fire from a surrounding building, he took him to a safe place where a medic could attend to him. Later, when his company had to go into a row of houses to flush out insurgents, Osvaldo was shot, but his body armor saved him. He was experiencing anger, fear and terror, but tried to remain emotionally withdrawn so that witnessing injuries or death would not bother him too much. At another time, while patrolling the street, an improvised explosive device (IED) went off nearby. He fell and struck his head and suspected he may have sustained a concussion. He felt dizzy and later started having headaches. Osvaldo was also anxious, had nightmares and could not sleep for days at a time. He was taken to a local military hospital where he was diagnosed as having a traumatic brain injury with PTSD and anxiety. He was declared unfit for combat and was sent home to seek treatment at a local VA hospital. While happy to return home to his wife and son, he found it difficult to adjust to civilian life. He had flashbacks and outbursts of anger. He was emotionally withdrawn, avoided socializing, and had trouble expressing feelings for his family. Though he recognized he was depressed, he was reluctant to seek psychiatric treatment for fear that he would be perceived as weak. One of his friends gave him opioids which temporarily made him euphoric and helped him forget about his traumatic experiences. However, Osvaldo found that he felt more depressed after the opioids wore off. So he stopped taking the drugs and decided to seek psychiatric treatment. I placed him on an SSRI antidepressant to treat his PTSD, depression and anxiety, carbamazepine for anger and a non-habit forming sedative for insomnia. His minor headaches and dizzy spells were resolved with the help of a neurologist. I also referred him to our psychologist for psychotherapy and substance abuse counseling. His wife was supportive, and he was well motivated. A few months of cognitive behavior therapy and exposure therapy (gradual exposure to feelings, thoughts, and events associated with his war-related trauma to reduce level of distress) helped relieve Osvaldo's symptoms of PTSD and anxiety. The therapist also taught him how to relax with mindfulness meditation. This helped him focus and deal with the present calmly instead of thinking of the traumatic past or the fearful future. He also started attending group therapy sessions with other Iraq war vets, finding comfort in the fact that many had problems similar to his. It was comforting that he was not facing these problems alone and he benefited from their experiences and success stories. He made new friends in the group and gained strength from their support and understanding.

After a few months of psychiatric treatment his PTSD symptoms lessened. He recovered from his depression and he was less anxious and slept better. His interpersonal relationships improved, he spent more time with his wife and child, and he started socializing more with his family and friends. He had retired from the army and our VA vocational counselor helped him find a suitable job. Osvaldo thanked us for helping him.

In the beginning, I had to get used to the VA bureaucracy, but overall, I enjoyed my work there. I was allotted one hour with a new patient, enough time to take a thorough psychiatric history, do a mental status examination, make a tentative diagnosis and devise a treatment plan. Some patients came with initial social histories done by our able social workers who had already seen them in primary care settings. I was fortunate to work with a dedicated mental health staff, most of whom were talented, hardworking and knowledgeable. They specialized in PTSD, substance abuse, depression, psychosis, and so on. The staff also helped veterans find jobs, acquire vocational skills, and address legal issues. Being a team player was key to working with a large diversified group. One of my talented and friendly physician assistants helped me prepare powerpoint slides on mental health topics like PTSD, depression and substance abuse. Without his help I would not have been able to give these presentations. I enjoyed giving lectures to the mental health staff, as well as to the whole hospital staff during grand rounds. While researching and preparing for these presentations, I gained valuable clinical knowledge myself, making me a better psychiatrist and a greater help to the veterans. Most veterans were grateful for getting good care at this VA hospital.

One of the downsides of working for the VA was that in the initial years the salary was not competitive. In addition, there was a national shortage of psychiatrists and few wanted to locate to a rural VA hospital like ours. We had only two or three psychiatrists in the mental health department for many years. One week out of every three, I was on a consultation call, including evenings and weekends, to manage psychiatric patients coming to the emergency room. Some veterans would get drunk and come to the emergency room in the middle of the night; some had thoughts of harming themselves or others. It was a challenge to assess and treat these patients and, at times, it was hard to find a bed in another VA hospital to refer a patient for inpatient psychiatric treatment. But eventually we did find a bed.

Initially, we documented patient histories and treatment plans by hand on a chart. After a few years, the VA switched to computerized patient records, lab orders, and prescriptions. All of which were entered and ordered by the physicians. I had to go to a local school to acquire typing skills and sometimes I found myself sitting next to one of my patients in class! They were surprised to see me there. Many senior staff had to go through a similar learning curve.

On the up side, working at a VA hospital meant that I did not have to deal with health insurance companies, managed care, or the inherent paperwork that has led to burnout in many non-VA physicians. Some of these non-VA physicians feel more bureaucrats rather than caring doctors and feel that they are not able to spend quality time with their patients. I also did not have to practice defensive medicine due to malpractice issues. Unlike in private practice, I did not have to deal with managing and hiring staff, meeting overhead expenses, or collecting fees from patients. I was just happy to receive my monthly check from Uncle Sam.

I was happy to help many veterans with mental health problems during my career at the VA hospital. My service line chiefs and colleagues were generally satisfied with my performance. I had formed a close relationship with several of my mental health colleagues and it was difficult to part with them when I decided to retire. We still keep in touch. I had also formed a close bond with many veterans, some of whom I had been seeing for more than fifteen years. Some cried when I told them that I was going to retire, but I had taken steps to assure their continued care by giving them notice months in advance and referring them to my trusted colleagues. I was going to miss them too. I was given a Certificate of Appreciation for completing seventeen years of service to the VA hospital. It was a nice gesture. This helped give me closure in recognizing that I had finally arrived! Looking back, I can see how far I've come in crossing countries and meeting many of my personal and professional challenges. I am grateful that my hard work and dedication has paid off. My hope is that I've made some positive impact along the way.

CHAPTER 20

SHILPI

Shilpi's Dental School Graduation
from West Virginia University

My youngest daughter, Shilpi, was growing up. She adored Shefali and being quite observant, she tried the same mischiefs that her older sister had from time to time. She did not always like to go to my favorite state parks with me, but she enjoyed making frequent trips to the mall with Meena. She joined the track team, like her sister, and ran the 800-meter and one mile race in an inter school meet. She had a tough time finishing the race due to fatigue, but she was determined; huffing and puffing, she finished second from last. We were proud of her perseverance and determination. These traits were going to be useful during her pursuit of higher education. She formed close friendships with a few girls in her class and from early childhood. They still reunite once a year, though they live far apart. Shilpi was well-liked in school and, similar to her sister, she was nominated to Prom Court by her peers and also participated in the Homecoming Parade. She received academic awards during her high school years at Woodrow Wilson High School, where her grades earned her a scholarship and honors status in the undergraduate program at West Virginia University.

Once at WVU, Shilpi majored in Biology and minored in Business Administration. She was unsure if she wanted to pursue dentistry or accounting. While she was doing her undergraduate studies, her brother-in-law, Pranav, was doing his orthodontic residency. She spent many of her evenings studying with him while he did lab work for his training. This early exposure to the dental field left an impression on her. She realized she liked the artistic and scientific components of the field and, inevitably, chose to strive for dental school. She felt she could apply both disciplines in her future dental practice. Luckily, Shilpi seemed to be less distracted by the WVU party scene than her sister seemed to have been, as she was able to maintain pretty good grades even from the beginning! Despite working hard and performing well, she was not receiving the highest marks in her classes. Because acceptance into dental school was highly competitive, this was stressful for her. But, like me, Shilpi was hard working and focused.

Shilpi met her future husband her freshman year of college in the honors dormitory at WVU, where they had mutual friends and classes. It was not until they were chemistry laboratory partners that they became close friends and eventually started dating. Arpan was on a premedical track, and both spent countless hours studying, shadowing, and doing lab research throughout their undergraduate career. Shilpi applied to WVU dental school and was waitlisted. Fortunately, after retaking the Dental Aptitude Test (the dental entrance exam), she improved her score and gained admittance into the WVU School of Dentistry, while Arpan proceeded on to medical school.

During her busy dental school years, Shilpi undertook a one-week mission trip to Guatemala. Exposure to the substandard living conditions of her patients made her appreciate the amenities and comforts we Americans enjoy. Since they did not trust the local drinking water, she and her colleagues drank the safer local bottled beer, Gallo. It was there that she developed a taste for beer and charitable dentistry.

Meena and I attended her dental graduation ceremony in Morgantown, WV in 2004. Shilpi asked Pranav, now an orthodontist, to do the honor of hooding her at the ceremony. It was important to her because of their family connection and his positive influence on her career choice. Shilpi had the biggest smile on her face when she received her diploma. My brother and his wife also attended to cheer her on. We were all very proud of her achievements.

Following her dental school, Shilpi applied and was accepted to the hospital-based general practice residency (GPR) program at the University of Texas in Houston. While Arpan began his ophthalmology residency in Kentucky, Shilpi left for Houston to begin her GPR. She immediately fell in love with the big city, a welcome change from living in a small town for many years. There, she made new friends and frequented many good restaurants. She lived with one of her oldest childhood friends from WV. This helped her transition to living outside of WV, where she had lived most of her life. During her residency year, she learned how to provide dental treatment for medically compromised patients in both outpatient and inpatient clinical settings.

After finishing her GPR, the couple set a wedding date of August 6, 2005. She had grand ideas of a fancy wedding in Chicago or Washington, D.C., in one of their many fine hotels. Beckley would not do because it had neither a hall big enough nor resources to cater good Indian food. We settled on Charleston, the capital of WV, which was a one hour drive from Beckley, where Arpan grew up, and where his parents still lived. Meena and I traveled there many times during the year to prepare for the wedding. Arpan's parents, Udyotji and Asha, helped us with the planning. We were very thankful to them for their help. We blocked a set of rooms at the Embassy Suites for our wedding guests and reserved their big ballroom for the musical event which was to take place the evening before the wedding, as well as for the dinner and reception for the next evening.

The couple wanted to follow traditional Indian wedding rituals, which included the celebratory welcoming parade of the groom's wedding party known as the baraat. Since the Embassy Suites Hotel was located on a busy downtown street, we could not arrange for Arpan to arrive on horseback as Pranav had done in India. So, it was decided that the wedding itself would be held at a country club just outside of Charleston, where Arpan could arrive on a horse and look regal, wearing a turban and carrying a sword, down a small country road. The horse had to be mildly sedated so that it would not get excited by the loud music and run away with Arpan!

This wedding expense far exceeded my budget, but I reluctantly agreed to please Shilpi and Meena. Shilpi was too busy in her own residency to plan the wedding, so she relinquished all control of the wedding details to Meena and her sister, Jyotsna. Our whole family helped us out with wedding arrangements in one way or another. For example, our nephew, Kuntal, took care of assigning the hotel rooms and arranged for transportation for our guests. My brother's wife, Reeta and her sister, helped create the beautiful flower arrangements. As one may imagine, the only detail that Shilpi and Arpan were particular about were the drinks to be selected for the reception and for the musical and traditional dance (garba) event. Unfortunately, they did not concede to my suggestion of a nonalcoholic wedding, but a good time was had by all. We decided to have a live singing group for the garba, and the men and women came dressed in their colorful Indian outfits ready to dance the night away. It was a wonderful event to celebrate with cherished family and friends.

We were excited to have so many important family members attend Shilpi's wedding. My mother was very excited that she could witness this beautiful wedding of her granddaughter in America. It was a dream come true for her. Many relatives even traveled from India. Meena's family was well represented by her sister and her husband, Jyotsna and Asheet, along with their daughter, Kanisha, and son Kuntal, who already lived in the states. Her uncles, Devendra, Sharad, Aunt Bhanu, and her cousin, Devang, also came from India. My brother Mukesh's family came from California and my sister Anupama's family came from Boston to attend the wedding. We were also happy to host Arpan's extended family and friends to be a part of all the festivities.

On her wedding day, following the musical baraat, Shilpi was brought to the beautifully decorated mandap (a raised platform with pillars) in a palanquin, carried by her cousin-brothers, to join Arpan and begin the wedding rituals. During the ceremony, the Hindu priest translated the traditional Sanskrit wedding vows to English so that the audience, and Shilpi and Arpan, could understand what they were promising to one another. The wedding was followed by a reception in the evening and my son-in-law, Pranav, did a good job serving as the MC. Both of us fathers gave our individual speeches, and Shefali, with tears, gave her happy toast to the couple. Arpan's parents, Udyotji and Asha, and his brother, Darshan, seemed excited and happy about welcoming a daughter and a sister into their family, just as we were happy to welcome another son. The speeches were followed by a father-daughter dance to Louis Armstrong's "What a Wonderful World," chosen because it described the beauty of nature, the love for my daughter, and the wonderful people around us. Arpan and his mother, who we sadly eventually lost to cancer, joined us for this beautiful dance. The youngsters then continued to dance till the wee hours of the morning fueled by their youthful energy, great music, good friends, and a variety of alcoholic beverages. The whole family was very happy that the year-long efforts had paid off with God's help.

After the wedding, Arpan and Shilpi settled down in their first home, a small house in a suburb of Lexington, Kentucky. While Arpan continued his ophthalmology residency, Shilpi found a job as an assistant professor of dentistry, both at the University of Kentucky. Shilpi also volunteered to treat underprivileged Hispanic children in the broader Lexington area. Some Hispanic families had moved to Bluegrass Country to tend the horses and stables owned by families involved in competitive horse racing. Some were jockeys who rode thoroughbred horses, competing in popular races in Lexington and Louisville. Other families were there due to their skill and mastery of how to tend to crops and farm land. Many could not afford health or dental insurance or pay for their dental care. Shilpi traveled in a mobile dental clinic to reach remote areas. She enjoyed this work treating Hispanic children. She learned to speak Spanish a little more fluently from the classes held by the very students she was teaching through a club they established known as the Hispanic Student Dental Association. During her professorship, in addition to teaching classes, Shilpi mentored dental students, provided dental public health education and services to the community, and wrote a review article that was published in a reputable dental journal.

In 2007, Arpan moved to Chicago to subspecialize in his field for a retina fellowship at Northwestern University. Shilpi decided to specialize further as well, and applied for an endodontics residency at the University of Texas, Houston Dental Branch. She was one of approximately 150 applicants. Fortunately, she had good letters of recommendation due to her strong work ethic and she was offered one of the two positions in the residency program. Meena and I were extremely proud of our daughter, but at the same time, we were worried about her taking up the challenge. The three-year residency required sacrifice living apart from Arpan, and hard work, and determination. I had a long talk with her, questioning whether pursuing further studies at this stage of her life was the right choice, but she was determined and Arpan was very supportive.

Shilpi became pregnant with her first daughter while she was in her last year of her endodontic residency, while preparing for her grueling board examinations. Towards the end of her pregnancy, the long hours and stress were taking a toll on her health and the baby's development. The doctor placed her on bed rest and she was told to stop attending classes to keep her activity and stress levels down so as to not adversely affect the pregnancy. During her training, dentistry had still been a fairly male-dominated field. There was little support from the program for pregnancy, and since it was not a hospital or government based program, there were no mandates for time off for maternity leave. She was given two weeks maternity leave, and then would have to resume her normal schedule. Shilpi feared that the extra weeks of being out of the program for bedrest might prolong the length of time she would have to stay to complete her program requirements. This, in turn, would further extend the time by when she could join Arpan in Georgia, where he had now begun his private practice. We reassured her that she would be fine no matter what the future would hold with family support. Shilpi was not easily convinced. So, Shefali traveled to Houston and stayed with Shilpi during this time to make sure she stayed put!

My granddaughter, Sahana, was born in December, 2009. To our relief, she and Shilpi were both healthy following the pregnancy and delivery. Arpan visited as often as he could from Georgia, but his schedule was also very demanding. He was only able to fly to Houston about one weekend per month. When he was not present, Shilpi juggled being a full-time mother to Sahana and keeping up with the demands of her residency. Meena and I were comforted by the fact that Shilpi had two cousins nearby, Kuntal and Veeral, to support her if needed. Meena and Arpan's mother, Asha, made frequent trips to Houston to help take care of Sahana while Shilpi resumed her classes. While Shilpi studied for her board examination in the evenings, Veeral would come and babysit his niece after work. This went on for six months until they moved to Georgia. They were all a great support to her. Shilpi passed the board examination and finally finished her residency in 2010.

In July of 2010, Shilpi, Arpan, and Sahana were reunited and settled down in Macon, Georgia where they currently reside. Arpan had joined a private group practice and Shilpi started a solo practice in endodontics. When Arpan's mother passed away, his father moved to Macon, GA, as well. He wanted to be close to family and enjoy the sunny, warm weather the state has to offer, which is a stark contrast from the cold winters we all bore in WV. We are thankful to him for being a positive parental and grandfatherly presence in Shilpi and Arpan's family life.

Between Shilpi and Shefali, Meena and I are blessed to have a total of three beautiful granddaughters, Raya, Ayana, and Sahana. In 2012, Shilpi had a son, our beloved, Saavan. We are happy to see Shilpi and her family settled nicely in Macon and are proud of their and our grandchildren's achievements. We frequently make the six hour road trip to Macon and enjoy our time with them, especially playing with our grandkids.

Shilpi and Arpan's Wedding in Charleston, WV

CHAPTER 21

MOTHER AND FATHER

My mother had relocated to the US in 2003, two years after my father's death. After living with my brother and his wife, Mukesh and Reeta, she moved in with us in Beckley, WV. Ours was a two-story house that had a living room, bedroom and full bathroom downstairs. My mother's need for a walker, due to her severe arthritis, precluded her climbing the stairs, so we put a hospital bed in the living room for her. She was insecure and would panic if she was left on her own, even for an hour. She was concerned about her health and wanted someone around in case something happened to her. This made it difficult for Meena to go out to run errands or socialize. We eventually found a local Indian woman to keep her company during the day and take care of some of her needs. My former retired secretary, with whom we were still close, agreed to keep her company in the evening and slept in the adjoining bedroom. Despite my mother's history of having difficulty getting along with servants in India, to our surprise she seemed to get along with these helpers. This was a great relief for us. When we wanted to take a vacation or visit our kids, my brother and his wife, or my sister, Anupama, would come to stay.

Though my mother was mostly in my brother's and my care during her latter years, both of my sisters, Anupama and Shobhana, and their families have cared for my parents quite a lot as they began to get older and required more attention. Shobhana's children, Prashant and Jesal, who live in Mumbai were close to their grandparents and spent a lot of time with them growing up. Both of them are now married and each have a son of their own. They are doing well in their professional lives with Prashant working in finance and Jesal for an American company in information technology. My other sister, Anupama, who now lives in Boston, also has two sons with Rahul, the oldest, residing in Boston as well. He is a teacher and is active in coaching basketball. Like me, he has always had a passion for learning History. Anand, Anupama's youngest son, is now married with two young daughters of his own. He is busy with his family life and is a successful physician practicing Urology with a specialization in men's reproduction health in Chattanooga, TN. Along with my brother's three sons, my daughters, Shefali and Shilpi, are the only two girls. They always say how blessed they are to have so many cousin-brothers to be adored by! My mother and father cherished their grandchildren and enjoyed knowing what was happening in their lives. My mother was even lucky enough to spend some time with her great grand-children! They, in turn, enjoyed being able to spend time with her.

At home with us in Beckley, my mother had a daily routine. Her schedule consisted of breakfast, getting dressed (with help), and prayers and meditation. These prayers provided her both strength and peace. She enjoyed her Indian meal for lunch cooked by Meena and then would have a siesta. Her afternoons were spent cutting newspaper clippings, talking on the phone, reading, writing and watching some TV. Sometimes, I would take her to a state park or to visit friends. I remember watching TV programs every evening with her.

When my mother turned 90, my brother came to visit from his home in San Diego to celebrate with her. While she was cutting her cake, she informed us, "Listen Ramesh and Mukesh, I plan to live a hundred years, so be prepared to look after me for a long time!" She amused us often with her thoughts and quirky ways. Our children and grandchildren visited her as often as they could as well. She looked forward to their visits and they enjoyed each other's company despite the language barrier. Instead of talking, she would sit and have them help her with whatever creative project she was working on at the moment, like clipping pictures from magazines and newspapers. It was nice to have the kids be exposed to someone who carried the history and traditional ways of the older Indian generation because by now, we ourselves, had become more acculturated within the American lifestyle. I believe, despite some of her disabilities, with all the caring she received from the people around her that my mother enjoyed her life.

She was hospitalized repeatedly for heart (cardiac) problems. After one such hospitalization she was put in a nursing home for rehabilitation. She had become so weak that she had to be confined to a wheelchair, unable to use her walker any longer. She needed help with even the most basic activities and was in no condition to return home. After an initial stage of anger and denial, she eventually accepted the fact that she would have to stay for an extended period in the nursing home. After a few months, she was moved to a private room. Each day, she looked forward to Meena bringing her home cooked meals. She soon adapted to her surroundings, and though she did not speak proper English, she was friendly and quite popular with the nursing home staff.

She kept herself busy, in general, in spite of not taking part in the nursing home activities like cards or bingo. I tried to visit her every other day and took her out on the weekends. I remember when I used to put her in her wheelchair and push her past other patient rooms, she would announce loudly in her broken English, "My son. Doctor." Though somewhat embarrassing, it was nice to see her communicating with her American peers and hear her have pride for me. I was impressed by her ability to adjust to new environments in a country to which she was not accustomed. Though lacking higher education, she had good common sense and emotional strength and learned that she could survive, with our help, after years of being dependent on my father who had taken very good care of her.

I was planning to retire from the VA hospital in the fall of 2015. Meena and I were having difficulties handling the long cold winters of West Virginia and were considering moving to the sunny southern state of Florida. My mother expressed a desire to be near my younger brother, Mukesh, in San Diego. So, he and his wife, Reeta, applied to get her admitted to a good nursing home facility near their home. My brother then came to Beckley to accompany her on the plane ride to San Diego.

By the fall of that year, Meena and I had moved to an active retirement community in central Florida.

Mukesh, the youngest and, he would say, the handsome one of the family, joined my sister, Anupama, and me to live in the states. He arrived at the age of 23 during the blizzard of 1978 and attended the University of Illinois in Urbana Champagne. Weathering through the adventures of a new country, climate, and culture, Mukesh finished his Master's Degree in electrical engineering and landed a job in Dayton, Ohio. Anupama still lived there at the time and I was not too far away finishing my residency in Columbus, so I was thrilled to have both my siblings close by! Soon after in 1981, Mukesh fell head over heels in love and within five weeks, married his wife, Reeta. Together, they have lived in many places from California, Oregon, Virginia, and back to California, where they now live in beautiful Del Mar, San Diego. Along the way, they had three sons, who I am proud to see succeeding in very different professions.

Akshay, the oldest son born in 1984, is currently a film producer in Hollywood, having done productions like "American Standoff" and documentaries that shed light on the plight of refugees around the world. Ankur, the mischievous middle child, followed more in his dad's footsteps having worked in the geo-mapping industry, and now, electrical transmission design. Akeel, the baby of the family, pursued his mother's line of interest in hospitality management and helped bring two startup restaurants to Michelin Star status, Lazy Bear in San Francisco (2-Stars) and Single Thread in Sonoma (3-Stars). I am excited to see what else these young men will accomplish.

Mukesh, Reeta, and their sons helped my mother in her transition to San Diego by finding her a nice nursing home that had a beautiful view of the ocean and visited her often. She gradually became accustomed to her new home. She shared a room with one woman and shared a bathroom with three others. She was quite friendly with the nursing home staff who were from a variety of places with their own unique dialects. On one of my visits she said, "Ramesh, I am so lucky. Who knew that I would come to the US, thousands of miles from home, and meet so many nice people from different nationalities?" Besides her broken English, she had picked up some words of Spanish. I was impressed by her positive attitude.

In May of 2015, thanks to the planning by Mukesh and Reeta, our family held a Shah Family Reunion in a beachfront home in San Diego. My children, Shefali and Shilpi, my grandchildren, and most of my siblings with their kids and grandchildren, as well as some extended family, all joined for an enjoyable retreat together. We brought my mother from the nursing home and she thoroughly enjoyed everyone's company and attention. Our grandchildren were especially happy to share time and love with their ninety-year-old grandma. It was a warm and joyous family gathering.

One Christmas, Meena and I had planned to visit our children and grandchildren in Georgia in 2016. But, we decided to visit my mother in San Diego instead because of her deteriorating health. When we arrived, she had swelling and ulcers on her legs which were not responding to treatment. She was breathless and anxious, and said that she missed us. She wanted to come visit us in Florida, but we knew that she was in no shape to travel. We had extended talks with her, thinking that we might never talk to her again. After a few days we returned to Florida, and a week later she passed away at the age of ninety-two. Her optimistic attitude, despite overwhelming odds, was admirable. She taught us to face aging with positivity, courage and adaptation.

My mother's death caused me to reflect on my childhood, my father and my ancestors. In the mid-19th century, my great-grandfather, Mulchand, lived in the semi-desert land of Kutch, which is now a part of Gujarat. It lies in the western part of India, bordering Pakistan, approximately 1300 miles from Kerala. He was a wealthy landlord and when he died his only son, Shantidas (my paternal grandfather), was just a teenager. According to family lore, some relatives took my great-grandfather's land, leaving my grandfather penniless. He then migrated to Bombay (now Mumbai) where he found work as a laborer. He saved enough money to open a small clothing store and began investing in the stock market, mainly in the cotton exchange. He eventually settled in the small town of Dhulia In Maharashtra where he married and fathered five sons and three daughters. My father, Chamanlal, was the second son. My grandfather wanted both his eldest sons to work in the shop, but only the oldest son, Himatlal, did so. My father, Chamanlal, and his younger two brothers, Daulat Kumar and Chandrakant, pursued higher education in business, medicine and engineering, while the three sisters, Indu, Leela and Bhanu, had arranged marriages and settled in Mumbai.

My father was quite brilliant and obtained a scholarship to a commerce college in Ahmedabad, Gujarat. He earned a bachelor's degree, and in 1942 married my mother, Manidevi, through arrangement. My mother was born in Kutch Mandvi, a thriving port on the Arabian Sea which borders Pakistan. Her father had married twice, the second time to my maternal grandmother after his first wife passed away. The first wife bore three daughters and one son; the second wife, three daughters. My maternal grandfather traveled overseas in sailboats called "dhows" to faraway ports like Seychelles and Aden in the Indian Ocean to further his business. He had accumulated some wealth by the time he passed away, when my mother was only two years old. This left my grandmother, a young widow, with many children to support. My mother's anxiety, episodes of depression, and paranoia, which plagued her even in her adult life, may have partly been the result of growing up fatherless. She had only a high school education, spoke Gujarati and very little English, and was highly dependent on my father.

The whole family moved to Madras (Chennai) in south India, shortly after my birth in 1944. My father obtained a job in a bank, his commerce degree being a rarity in the Gujarati Jain community. Our community was known as the Gujarati Jain Bania community from Kutch. Gujaratis are a business community and some of them have established big businesses, not only in India, but abroad as well. Like my father, many Gujaratis have migrated to other parts of India and the world in search of expanding their business and trade opportunities. Recently, many Gujaratis have moved to Europe and the US to pursue careers as doctors, engineers and businessmen. Gujaratis generally practice either Hinduism or Jainism, a pacifist religion with an emphasis on ahimsa (nonviolence). Mahatma Gandhi also was a Gujarati Hindu who practiced ahimsa and utilized the weapon of nonviolence against the British in India's Freedom Movement.

Gujarat is a coastal state and carries out maritime trade with other parts of India, Africa and the Middle East countries. Gujaratis have been sailing to those parts of the world for 150 years. They usually traveled in sailboats sometimes taking weeks to reach their destinations.

My mother's relatives were settled in Calicut, Kerala and had both an umbrella manufacturing factory (mostly assembling) and a soap factory. They were looking for a manager with a commerce degree and my father was offered the job. Thus, in 1946, we ended up in Kerala. Because of heavy rains from June to September umbrella sales were good. During those years there was no competition from China or Japan flooding Indian markets with their goods. The small soap factory produced "vegetable soaps" (no animal lard) in accordance with our vegetarian Jain faith. The labor unions were strong and were often supported by ruling state communist governments. So, it was not unusual for the laborers to go on strike for higher wages and picket for weeks at a time. However, my father was emotionally strong and faced these strikes with courage. After some negotiation, management and the labor union would reach a compromise and umbrella production would resume.

My childhood, until the age of eleven, was spent in Calicut. I was the oldest of five children: three sons and two daughters. My youngest brother, Kamlesh, died tragically at the age of four in an accident while playing. This was a shock to my parents, and they grieved over his death for many years. My father worked many hours for little income in the initial years. My parents were stressed, trying to settle down in this new south Indian state with an alien language and culture.

Like most Indian parents, mine were strict disciplinarians. I recall being scolded and receiving some spankings for being quite naughty and hyperactive. Initially, I was sent to a Gujarati school for four years and then to a Catholic school. I remember a priest roaming the corridors with a bible in one hand and a cane in the other. If he caught us breaking school rules, he would cane us in our hand. My sisters, Anupama and Shobhana, were educated in a local Catholic convent school. I spent a lot of time playing with my cousins. Those were happy times. We played soccer without shoes, cricket and other Indian games, such as Kabadi. I also remember rearing some pigeons. My brother, Mukesh, 10 years younger than me, was sent to the beautiful Blue Mountains School, a non-military school in the Nilgiris Mountains.

My parents then moved to Mysore in the nearby state of Karnataka in 1979. They relocated to open another umbrella factory because of continued problems with the labor union in Calicut, Kerala. There my parents built a beautiful house which they anointed "Kamal Kunj," so named for my youngest brother, Kamlesh. They lived there happily for many years.

In 1999, my father was having difficulty breathing, a chronic cough and tiredness so he consulted a pulmonologist who diagnosed him as having interstitial pulmonary fibrosis (IPF) of the lungs. This causes the lungs to become stiff and thick. At that time there was no known cure or treatment for this dreadful disease. He continued with the prescribed medications, but he wanted to go to his birthplace, Dhulia, where his family resided including his brother and his wife, Daulatkumar and Vanmala, both of whom were physicians. Daulatkumar, too, suffered from another serious lung disease. It was difficult to hear both of these very accomplished and respected men coughing loudly and sounding breathless. Once a tall, strong man, my father had lost a lot of weight and became weak. I had to push him in a wheelchair to get him on a train back to Mumbai. We spent the next few weeks in an apartment in Mumbai next to my sister and her husband, Shobhana and Chandrasen, and their two sons, Prashant and Jesal. My parent's apartment was located on the sixth floor of a high rise. When the day of my departure back to the US arrived, I was feeling sad because I was not sure whether I would see him again. My father insisted on coming down to the ground floor to bid me goodbye, despite him being very weak and short of breath. He told me "Ramesh, I wanted to let you know that you are a gem of a boy." Those parting words meant a great deal to me.

When I returned to the States, I began inquiring about a cure for IPF of lungs. I talked to a research physician at John Hopkins Hospital. After explaining my father's history and current deteriorated health, he did not feel that my father was a candidate for either an experimental drug or a lung transplant. Just as well, since I later learned that the experimental drug trial had failed. It was difficult for me to give this information to my father, who was now back in Mysore, his hometown. He continued to deteriorate, becoming only skin and bones. My sisters took good care of him in the last few weeks of his life and gave moral and physical support to my mother. When I heard that he was nearing the end of life, I made airline reservations but arrived too late, a day after his funeral. My brother, Mukesh, had left the day before me and was able to see my father for a few hours before he died. I was able to participate in the prayer service the next day and spend time with my grieving mother and siblings. I wish I had arrived earlier to have proper closure with him. After a few days I returned home.

*   *   *

My tenure in Beckley allowed me greater leisure time than I had experienced previously. I enjoyed the slower pace of work with enough time to see outpatients. I was somewhat exhausted after many years of intensive training and difficult examinations, one after another. These years were full of stress and anxiety. But in Beckley I felt I could relax and take care of myself and my family.

I loved the outdoors, especially nearby Grandview State Park, with its mountainous trail overlooking a gorge where the New River flowed. Both, there and at Pipestem State Park, I enjoyed observing the greenery and wildlife. The Appalachian Mountains cover the entire state and they are at their most beautiful from May to November. The green leaves of the various species of trees change their color in the fall to yellow, flaming red, and brown and the whole state earns its befitting slogan "Wild and Wonderful West Virginia." Wildflowers color the mountainsides and rhododendrons bloom in the spring giving the parks a magnificent look. I, being a nature lover, would hike the mountains throughout the year on my own and enjoy being away from other human beings. I was reminded of a quotation by Indian poet laureate and Nobel Prize winner, Rabindranath Tagore, "Trees are the earth's endless effort to speak to the listening heaven."

One of my favorite haunts was Little Beaver State Park. It has a tranquil lake where I would take my family paddle boating. Beautiful streams and small waterfalls added to the beauty. I would take my binoculars for bird watching and take photographs of cardinals, blue jays, robins, warblers, woodpeckers, eagles and ducks. I would meditate and feel the presence of God, the great creator, who was responsible for all the beauty I saw.

I also enjoyed playing golf with my buddies on the beautiful, mountainous golf courses. While my friends were concentrating on making birdies, I was busy admiring the trees, ponds, animals and birds. They were amused by my not seriously concentrating on my game.

The state would be blanketed with snow in the cold wintry months. I would go hiking in the state parks on sunny winter days dressed in layers of clothes. My family and friends thought I was crazy, but the combination of sunlight and snow would make the beautiful parks look like the cloud-filled heavens. The trees had shed their leaves and were coated with snow. The waterfalls and streams were frozen but beneath the ice, water would flow with a tranquil rippling sound. Again, I would be totally immersed in this winter wonderland, totally at peace. For some reason, in these surroundings, I could feel the bliss of the divine self within. I was somewhat sad to leave these beautiful Appalachian Mountains when we decided to move to the sunshine state of Florida.

I felt that living in Beckley was a gift. It was like living in a beautiful Indian hill station of my younger school days. In small towns, like Beckley, tight knit relationships are formed. Meena and I will always remember the good times we had with our different friendship circles, and the deep connections we formed among the simple and kind-natured people of Appalachia.

We listed our two-story home in Beckley, WV for sale in the summer of 2015. West Virginia was in an economic recession, partly due to less demand for coal. There were nearly seven hundred houses for sale in our Raleigh county alone. We were lucky to find a buyer within two months. Shefali and Shilpi traveled from Chicago, IL and Macon, GA with their families, one last time, to stay in the house where they had grown up. We all gathered in the living room and sang the song "Take Me Home, Country Roads" by John Denver. Tears were streaming down my younger daughter's face when we sang that song for the last time about her beloved West Virginia. They loved our Beckley home and were sad that they would not visit us there again. They did get to take their favorite furniture with them for memory sake since we were downsizing, and we pledged to hold a future family reunion in West Virginia.

My Father With My Cousins, Kirit, Satish
and Ashwin in Calicut, Kerala

My Parents, Siblings, Nephews, Meena, and Shilpi
at Shefali's Wedding in Mumbai, 1997

Friends Visiting My Mother in a Nursing
Home in Beckley, WV, 2013

CHAPTER 22

RETIREMENT IN FLORIDA

In front of Shantiniketan in Florida

While Meena and I were attending a spiritual seminar in Jacksonville, FL in the summer of 2014, we heard of an active adult retirement community called Shantiniketan, which means Abode of Peace. Shantiniketan is populated mostly by first generation Asian Indian immigrants, like us, over the age of 55. Just out of curiosity, we decided to visit this retirement community and take the two-hour drive to Tavares, Florida, a picturesque town, about 30 miles north of Orlando in Lake County. We found that Shantiniketan has three gated communities in short distance of one another and that each one consists of rows of condominiums to house an individual or a couple. The third gated community has plans to also have individual housing units as well.

The community was developed by Indian entrepreneur and engineer, Iggy Ignatius, who is from Michigan. During his travels all over the US, talking to senior Indians, he discovered that there was a need for such a community in a warm climate. Despite initial financial setbacks during the 2008 economic meltdown, courageous Iggy continued to build condos. When we visited, he had already completed phase one, consisting of about fifty condos, and they were sold out. The 1,200 square feet condominiums consisted of two bedrooms, two baths, a great room, kitchen and an attached one car garage. The community had a central clubhouse with a commercial grade kitchen which employs three full-time cooks specializing in delicious vegetarian Indian cuisine. During our visit we met some of the residents, mostly retired professionals and their spouses. A couple of the residents were gracious enough to show us around the area, to include a couple of beautiful lakes nearby. Meena immediately liked the community and felt that we should put down a deposit. At that time, only two rows of condos had been completed in phase two. She was mostly comforted to know that, should anything happen to her, I would be well fed; especially since I did not know how to cook! We would also be among like-minded, retired professionals.

By the fall of that same year, I had retired from the VA hospital and we had sold our Beckley home. Since we were downsizing, we had to sell off a lot of our furniture and clothes. Meena had two garage sales, our daughters took some furniture, and the rest we gave away to charity. We sadly parted with our Beckley friends, whom we had known for thirty years, at a farewell party at a local restaurant.

The next day we began our journey from Beckley to Tavares, me in our 2004 model Acura sedan and Meena in the newer Lexus SUV. After an overnight stay in Charlotte, North Carolina we continued south on the heavily traveled, three lane highway, I-75. When I heard a strange noise coming from the road, I assumed it was caused by road construction and continued to drive in the center lane at 70 mph. As soon as we crossed into South Carolina there was a blowout in my front left tire. Smoke came from the tire and the car started wobbling. I had the presence of mind not to panic. There was a hard shoulder on either side of the road but since there was a car coming behind me in the left lane, I decided to move over to the right. The car in the right lane behind me slowed down, and I gradually maneuvered my car to the right shoulder. I could have been seriously injured or killed by a vehicle traveling at a high speed. Meena pulled her car a little distance away from me and came to my side. My heart was pounding, and the traffic continued to speed past. Since I did not know at which mile marker my car was parked, I decided to call 911 instead of AAA. They connected me to a deputy sheriff who took down all of the details and said that help would be on the way shortly. After fifteen long minutes a service truck pulled in behind me with lights flashing. He replaced the flat tire with the temporary one from the trunk and suggested that I take the next exit and find a tire store where I could purchase a full-size tire. He would not accept any money stating that it was a free service offered by the South Carolina state to stranded motorists. I thanked him for his kind service. It took about two hours to replace the temporary tire and despite some anxiety, I again headed south on I-75 with Meena following close behind. On the way I had another tire punctured by a nail which we had repaired in Savannah, Georgia. Finally, with God's grace we reached Tavares safely one day later. I was carrying two marble statues of Indian deities in the trunk, perhaps they were looking out for me like angels. Anyway, we were just happy to reach our destination safe and sound.

We took legal possession of our new condo and since we had no furniture, we visited furniture stores in Lake County and Orlando. We set a land speed record and furnished our condo in just two days. We started making new friends, many of whom were transplants like us from northern snow belt states like Michigan, Ohio, Maryland, Massachusetts, Illinois and New Jersey. Many of them were "snowbirds," visiting Florida from October to April when the weather was generally cool and comfortable. Those of us who stay year-round are referred to as "sunbirds." The heat is a factor and it is not unusual for the summer temperatures to hit the 90s for weeks at a time. We would get early evening rain for about an hour each day. So, all outdoor activities are done either in the early morning or late evening when the temperatures are more moderate. We spend the rest of the time in air conditioning. Because we are surrounded by several lakes, we experience less humidity than southern Florida. What we like most is that it is sunny almost every day, reminding us of the weather in India. Daily sunshine and greenery just perks us up. We certainly do not miss the cold wintery months of West Virginia, but I do miss the beautiful mountains.

Lizards, small love bugs and innocuous insects abound in summer. Semi-tropical fauna and green trees such as magnolias and crepe myrtle dot the landscape. During my morning walks, I admire the many different colored roses and other beautiful flowers. Our residents with a green thumb grow different types of vegetable plants and fruits, such as bitter gourd, beans, okra mangoes and papayas. Meena and I often visit the serene Lake Dora to enjoy the sunset. It is a good time to meditate and observe the evening sky full of beautiful colors. I am reminded of another of Tagore's quotes "Clouds come floating into my life, no longer to carry rain or usher storm, but to add color to my sunset sky."

It was interesting, but not surprising, to meet many first-generation Indian immigrants like ourselves. About three million individuals of Indian origin reside in the US. More immigrants from India started arriving during President Johnson's era after 1965. Most immigrants are doctors, engineers, scientists, academics, businessmen or computer specialists. The American Association of Physicians of Indian origin (AAPI), of which I am a member, represents a conglomeration of more than 80,000 practicing physicians in the US. This organization is involved in charitable, educational and political activities. Many Indian American physicians have become famous: Vivek Murthy, former surgeon general, Sanjay Gupta, CNN medical reporter, Dilip Jeste, former president of the American Psychiatric Association, and authors Deepak Chopra, Abraham Varghese, Atul Gawande, and Siddhartha Mukherjee. There are also many Indian-owned private pharmacies. Thus, Indians are filling a vital need in the healthcare system.

Indian Americans have become prominent in several fields. Nicki Haley, former US ambassador to the United Nations, Bobby Jindal, former Governor of Louisiana, and Seema Verma, administrator of the centers for Medicare and Medicaid services in the Trump administration have achieved political fame. There are also an impressive number of Indian American business executives: Indra Nooyi, former CEO of PepsiCo and now on the board of directors of Amazon, Satya Nadela, CEO of Microsoft, Sundar Pichai, CEO of Google, Arvind Krishna CEO of IBM and Vikram Pandit, former CEO of Citigroup. Astrophysicist Subramanian Chandrasekhar won the Nobel Prize in physics. Priyanka Chopra and Dev Patel have achieved Hollywood fame.

Many Indians immigrated from the western states of Gujarat (known as Gujaratis), Maharashtra and South India. Many Gujaratis, like Patels, entered the hospitality industry and own many motels. I enjoy talking to our residents who come from different backgrounds. Their stories are fascinating; many of them come to the US with eight dollars in their pocket and have become successful in various fields.

Our housing association is governed by an elected board of residents. Most of the work is done by a salaried manager with the help of the board members who organize activities, oversee the maintenance of the common grounds, see to resident complaints and requests, and run the food club, etc. I was elected to the board this year and I am also the member of the health committee. I look forward to serving this retirement community and already, in the wake of the recent Corona Virus Pandemic, we have been active in ensuring the safety of our residents. There is a second manager for food service who also oversees the three Indian cooks and helpers. The buffet style vegetarian meals are served in the clubhouse and represent delicious cuisine from all over India. The lunch and dinner menus are prepared a month in advance and the residents have a choice of eating either spicy, non-spicy or Jain food (without root vegetables). Non-spicy food suits me. We have many residents who volunteer to help with the housing association or the food club activities. They do a good job and we are grateful to them. Our residents are required to follow the written rules of the association. Except for minor squabbles, most residents get along with each other.

Because senior citizens have to take extra care during the present Covid-19 outbreak, the health committee has temporarily stopped group activities and gatherings from happening. This is a necessary precaution for now, but Meena and I are looking forward to resuming life and socializing with others. In normal times, besides walking many miles with her friends, Meena is also involved with women's group activities, playing cards, bingo, discussion groups and yoga. She also volunteers her services to help other residents in need. Since I eat in the association's club house, it allows Meena to do minimal cooking in our own condo's small kitchen. She said, "I want to retire with Ramesh and not do much." It looks as if her desires have been satisfied as well and she has retired in the real sense of the word!

Besides walking, I play ping pong in the evening in our small gymnasium. Occasionally I play golf in the winter. The golf courses around here are not as green as West Virginia. I spend a few hours a day writing or playing bridge with my friends. The residents also take bus trips to nearby state parks, beaches or other places of interest such as the Kennedy Space Center. Meena serves as one of the organizers and does a good job. We also visit the malls and restaurants in nearby Orlando on the weekends.

The multi-faith prayer room has a daily schedule of religious activities like reading scriptures or singing of hymns or "Bhajans." Religious and other holidays are celebrated with a party at least once a month. We have parties during Holi, Cinco de Mayo, Diwali, South Indian New Year's Day, Christmas and New Year's. The 9-day Navratri festival in October is celebrated with music and raas garba, our traditional Indian dance, each evening. This is followed by prayers honoring the Indian goddesses. Most residents take part in the festivities. Many residents throw birthday or anniversary parties. Meena and I celebrated our 50th wedding anniversary in the clubhouse in March of 2019. We both have faced our initial struggles with courage. Now we have settled down to a peaceful and happy married life. Both my daughters' families came to celebrate with us and gave speeches during our wedding anniversary. It was a joyous occasion.

Amateur singers in Shantiniketan have a chance to show off their talents on the stage every other Saturday evening. A health discussion group meets once a month where several physicians, including me, lead the discussion on health-related topics. I have given PowerPoint presentations to residents on topics such as depression, dementia and insomnia. Others have given talks on diabetes and healthy aging. This way we try to keep ourselves busy mentally, physically and socially.

Meena and I have also taken international trips to explore new countries and experience their culture. We have made trips to Europe, Africa, South America, Australia, New Zealand and India.

We have been fortunate to be able to travel the world so much. Because of my strong interest in history and geography, I have made this a priority in my life. Along the way I have had many memorable experiences and some, what I would call, misadventures. During one trip in March of 1999, we had made a trip with our two daughters and my son-in-law, Pranav, to the island of Kauai, one of the beautiful Hawaiian islands. It is also known as the garden island because of its lush greenery on one side of the island. Pranav and I had decided to go snorkeling off of Poipu Beach and in the waters of Kauai cove. We put on our snorkeling gear and waded into the waters of the cove. We had traveled some distance and were admiring the beautiful colorful fishes underwater. During that time a big black fish-like object as big as me brushed up on us and swam past. Not knowing what it was and frightened that it was a shark, we both made a quick turn around and swam as fast as we could back towards the beach where the rest of our family were sunbathing. We finally arrived on the shore huffing and puffing. As soon as we reached the beach we saw the big black animal that had brushed past us was actually a monk seal. It is an endangered species of seals and they are friendly creatures. It was lying on the beach with its belly up, flapping its fins and making strange noises. Once our hearts stopped racing, we all had a big laugh.

Kauai is also the home of a monastery dedicated to Lord Shiva, a Hindu God. This Shiva Temple is nestled serenely on a hill surrounded with beautiful Hawaiian trees, flowers and waterfalls. This hidden gem is also the home to the only sacred Rudraksha grove in the western world. The rudraksha are seeds from these trees that are used as prayer beads by devotees of Shiva for protection. I was surprised to find out that the head of the temple was a charismatic American swami, a religious

Hindu teacher or yogi, known at the temple as Subramaniam Swami. He was an actor in Hollywood before becoming a Hindu monk. He had traveled to South India, embraced Hinduism and became ordained as a swami there. One night, Subramanium Swami had a dream that he should build a Shiva Temple in Hawaii and thus, this temple was built. He had dreams of converting the temple into a golden temple, but he passed away before this could materialize. He was well versed in Hindu texts, including the Vedas, one of Hinduism's most ancient scriptures. He has also written a well illustrated book named "Dancing with Shiva." I was very impressed by his knowledge of Hinduism. This was a beautiful treasure to have found on our visit to Kauai.

During a different vacation in July of 2002, Meena and I had taken a Mediterranean cruise and one of its stops was in Barcelona, Spain. We took a shore excursion with the other passengers most of whom were also American. We set out to see the beautiful city of Barcelona by foot that is famous for its churches and buildings built by architect Antoni Gaudi. While walking around the city, I had secured a fanny pack to my belt beneath my jacket. In the pouch I had placed my passport and wallet that held my credit card and cash. I was walking on the street along with the other passengers when I was approached by a woman and her teenage daughter. The woman was holding a large cardboard in her hand and she and her daughter started begging for cash from me, while at the same time pushing me with her cardboard. I was sort of amused since I had seen these types of aggressive beggars in India. But I did not expect to find them in Europe. I told her in English to have patience and that I would give her a few dollars. Thankfully, a fellow passenger warned loudly, "Watch out! She has your wallet out!" I was so surprised that within such a short time they had been able to reach into my pouch, pull out my wallet and was about to run with it. Once they realized that I had caught them, they ran away. I felt so lucky and relieved that they did not get away with anything!

Another so-called misadventure I had was over the winter holidays in December 2002. Meena and I made a trip to Cancun, Mexico along with our two daughters, son-in-law Pranav, and my granddaughter Raya, who was only one and a half at the time. We settled down in a beautiful seaside resort. The next day my daughters, Pranav and I decided to take a snorkeling trip nearby in the Atlantic ocean. A Mexican man took us in a boat some distance away from the shore where plenty of fish abounded. We all wore a life jacket. He told us in broken English to jump in the water and he jumped in with us. The waves were fairly big and he told us to swim after him. We must have swam about 300 yards where he stopped and told us to look underwater with our snorkeling gear. We were delighted to see such exotic colorful fishes. Our guide also took a dive inside the ocean and came out with an eel in his hand proudly showing it to us. After that he told us to return to the boat. My daughters and Pranav were strong swimmers and were able to keep up with the guide. They reached the boat in no time despite the current of big waves coming against us. I was left behind and had a tough time swimming against the waves. I thought I would never reach the boat and became slightly panicked that I would drown. I signaled to them by raising my one arm high thinking that my kids would see me and come to my rescue. But they did not see me. Fortunately, I mustered all my strength, swam as hard as I could and finally reached our boat. When I started complaining my kids said, "Dad, you should have raised your arm!" I just gave them an exasperated look and then was just happy to be alive and with them on the boat.

More recently in January 2017, Meena and I decided to explore South America. The trip was arranged by a travel agency and a tour guide accompanied us throughout. Three other couples who were our close friends of ours from Beckley also joined us. After visiting Brazil and Argentina, we flew into the seaside city of Lima in Peru. The next day we took a small plane and landed in the Andes Mountains in a city known as Cusco. Cusco is located about 11,000 feet above sea level. We were housed in a beautiful hotel with modern amenities. But Meena and I started developing symptoms of altitude sickness. We had some difficulty in breathing, mild headaches, loss of appetite and nausea due to the thin mountain air. But we were trying to get used to it by drinking the cocoa tea that is supposed to help relieve some of these symptoms. I'm not sure that it helped us very much at all.

The following day we took a train ride through the beautiful Andes to the ancient Inca Indian settlement, Machu Picchu, which is one of the archeological wonders of the world. I was very excited to see it, but we had to climb steep hills and steps to see this settlement. I became more and more tired and had difficulty breathing, probably due to mountain sickness. But I continued and somehow managed. After seeing this amazing site we took the train ride back to Cusco. I was exhausted and was glad to hit the bed. However, in the middle of the night I woke up. I was breathless and my heart was beating fast. I felt very fatigued. Upon the advice of my physician friend, I took a small sedative and acetazolamide which I was carrying. I also requested the front desk to bring some portable oxygen to my room. But none of that made me feel much better and I had a restless sleep. I could not differentiate if I was having altitude sickness or whether I was experiencing anxiety. The travel guide called a Peruvian doctor who examined me. He said he could not guarantee that my symptoms would improve the next day when we were to continue our trip into the higher altitudes by bus. But he said I was fit enough to travel by plane back to Lima. Thereupon, Meena and I reluctantly decided to take a plane back to Lima just to ensure the safety of my health. When we landed in the oceanside town of Lima, I felt significantly better. The next day we flew back home to good old USA. I was glad to be home.

Though a bit nervous to travel internationally again, I decided to venture out and visit Africa. It was always a bucket list destination for me. During our trip, one of the places Meena and I visited was the Serengeti National Park in Tanzania in East Africa. We landed in a small strip airport in a two-seater plane near Serengeti after passing over Mount Kilimanjaro. Our local travel agents took us on a bumpy ride to an unfenced camp in the middle of the Serengeti jungle. The camp consisted of six small tents in the front for guests and a short distance behind us were six more small tents. Those tents housed the local African crew that was to look after us. We were scheduled to go on a Jeep safari the next day to see the wild animals of Africa. The tent had a bed, lanterns because of no electricity, and a commode. The water was provided by a small tank attached to the tent and at night we could zip the tent up.

The crew provided us with dinner in a bigger tent nearby. After dinner all of the guests gathered around a campfire. The guests included a family with children from France and an American couple from New Jersey. It was getting dark and the crew informed us to retire to our tents since a herd of wild buffaloes (different from American wild buffalos) were approaching us from afar. The crew captain warned us that since the camp was not fenced wild animals could come around, but they were unlikely to attack or harm us as long as we stayed inside our tents. Since our cell phones did not work there, they gave us a walkie-talkie to call one of the night crew in case of emergency. They also gave us a flashlight.

When Meena and I were about to sleep at 10pm we heard a strange sound just next to our tent. We soon figured out that it was a wild buffalo. He kept on grunting for an hour. We were just getting used to his grunts when we heard a lion roaring may be 100 yards away from us. I had only heard such a roar in the beginning of MGM movies before. We were frightened, but did not know what to do. Meena seemed less frightened than I was. The only weapon I had was a flashlight! I had my tent zipped up all the way, but the tent was so flimsy that I was sure the lion or buffalo could easily tear it up and come inside. Throughout the night we could hear the buffalos grunting and the lion roaring. I decided not to call the crew, since I knew that they were not allowed to carry guns and kill wild animals. Besides, the crew had informed us that we may hear wild animals at night. We kept praying the whole night and asked God to protect us. My faith in God got stronger that night! After an interrupted sleep, we were glad to see the rays of dawn even though it was still slightly dark. After cleaning up with the limited amount of water, I called for a crew member with my walkie-talkie and he arrived with a flashlight to accompany us to the big tent for breakfast. He flashed his light around our tent and said in a matter of fact voice that there was a wild buffalo behind our tent in the night and that it had just left. He also confirmed that there had also been a lion roaming around our camp as well. Most likely the lion was trying to hunt the buffalo and the buffalo was trying to hide by lying in between the tents. Boy, what an experience! We were glad to be safe and alive and with the night's excitement behind us, we were ready to begin our Jeep safari. During our African safaris in Serengeti, Masai Mara and Lake Elementaita National Parks, we were fortunate to see so many wild animals including the big five: elephants, lions, leopards, buffalos and rhinos. We certainly enjoyed our adventurous trip. But, needless to say, we will be opting to stay in a fenced camp on our next jungle expedition!

In addition to seeing new places, we also try to travel back to India every two years to visit Meena's mother, her sister Jyotsna, my sister Shobhana, and our extended families. We enjoy connecting with our extended family members at family reunions and have a good time together. Two years ago my class of 1967 Kasturba Medical College alumni reunion met in Cochin, Kerala, India which Meena and I attended. It was nice to connect with my classmates and reminisce about the good old days. They were aging nicely (including me) like old fine wine.

I have truly enjoyed my travels over the years. It was a necessary respite from my work so I could feel rested and rejuvenated enough to be able to return to my patients and practice without feeling burnt out or stressed. Taking time away also reinvigorated me mentally, physically, and spiritually. I have been fortunate to be able to vacation with family and friends as it gave us more time to know one another and improve upon our relationships. Traveling with grandchildren has been extra special as we are able to have more time to bond with them and pass on some of our elderly wisdom, values and beliefs.

While traveling around the world, Meena and I have come across many wonderful people from different countries and cultures. Their life experiences have given us guidance and insight in how to lead our own lives well. Learning about other cultures first hand has broadened our horizons, made us more open-minded and provided us a better understanding of how to treat people from other cultures and beliefs with tolerance and respect. After seeing the beauty of nature around the world it has made us nature lovers and advocates for preserving the earth, national parks and wildlife. Overall, I believe our travels and adventures around the world have enriched me and my family and have made us into better persons.

**At Lake Elementaita, Kenya, Africa with Jyotsna,
Asheet, Kuntal and Kanisha, 2019**

Shah Family Reunion in Outerbanks, North Carolina in 2012

Visiting with My Sister Shobhana (2nd from right)
and Paternal Cousins in Amravati, India, 2017

CHAPTER 23

RESIDENT STORIES

Ping Pong Team in Shantiniketan, Tavares, Florida

The majority of our residents have some minor physical problems, common in an older demographic population, and lead active lives in our independent retirement community. As expected, there are also a few residents who are suffering from severe physical disabilities or illnesses. I have learned a great deal about how these folks are facing their problems through observation and conversation with them.

One of our illustrious residents is retired Air Marshal Raghavendran (Nickname Raghu) from the Indian Air Force. He and his wife have been living near their daughters in New York for many years. They have spent their winters here for the past three years where one of their daughters resides with them. Though he celebrated his 90th birthday recently, Raghu is in good physical shape except for the loss of a significant amount of sight, back and knee problems. I am always impressed by how he carries on his daily life despite his handicap. He told me, "Regardless of having physical problems, one should have strength of mind. If life is manageable and one can do things, then one should have an optimistic attitude. I keep doing this physically and mentally. Life is God given, so we should not be depressed. I don't feel I have aged in my mind. My thinking and spirits are that of a thirty-five-year-old man. When I meet people at a Friday happy hour party or other parties, I want to be happy. I like to talk about enjoyable things, crack jokes and eat good food. Due to my severe eyesight problems I try to adapt by using magnifying gadgets. I have connected my laptop to a sixty-inch TV where I can magnify words and read them slowly. I can read newspapers with the help of magnifying glasses. I conduct discussion groups with the residents on ways to improve their lives. I enjoy keeping fit. Every day I do thirty minutes of cycling on a stationary bike and thirty minutes of strengthening exercises with machines in our gym. I have no regrets. I had a wonderful career in the Indian Air Force. I was the squadron leader and was not afraid of dying. But I was worried about what would happen to my family if I died."

As a psychiatrist, I recognize the many traits Raghu has which keep him fit and happy despite his age and disability. He is an optimist and an extrovert. He is interested in other people and enjoys having a good time. People like to be around him and enjoy conversing with him. He has many stories about the military and his extensive travels around the world. He was especially fond of traveling to holy places to learn about different religions. Besides traveling to most holy places in India he has also visited Israel and Karbala. He is open to new experiences, as well as meeting and getting to know people from different religious and ethnic backgrounds. It is obvious that he is a devoted family man who adores his wife who is also active and has been a constant source of support. Both are living examples of aging gracefully.

Another resident suffering from severe blindness and other physical problems is Dr. Dinish Patel. He is a highly knowledgeable retired geriatrician from Maryland. Despite his handicap he continues to play and teach bridge. He enjoys listening to music and is a good singer. Both he and I are members of the Shantiniketan Health Committee. He often speaks on various medical topics and I am impressed by his wealth of knowledge. His wife is supportive and is always at his side. She drives and takes him around. I have been surprised by his resilience in that he does not seem to allow his visual impairment to bring him down or hold him back in contributing and being involved in those activities he finds of interest. He has adapted really well.

Vijaya lived with her husband Srinivasan in the New York area. She had worked as an administrator in the long-term care and rehabilitation industry for forty years. Her husband worked as a senior civil engineer maintaining the Brooklyn Bridge. They are the proud parents of a talented and caring son and daughter. She believes in lifelong learning and purposefulness through service to others and making their lives better. In 2003, she was diagnosed with endometrial cancer. She underwent a hysterectomy which removed the whole cancerous growth and as a result she did not need chemotherapy. She faced her battle with cancer with courage and faith in God and, miraculously, has since been cancer free. However, she started having a chronic cough and shortness of breath in 2010 and by February 2012 she was diagnosed with Interstitial Pulmonary Fibrosis. She continued to work as a nursing home administrator carrying her oxygen tank with her. Her staff was distressed to see her suffer and many of her staff members prayed for her in their church. She inspired them to be brave and have faith in God. Eventually, she and her husband retired due to her illness. Her husband is her constant support. When her condition worsened, she consulted a lung transplant surgeon at the University of Pennsylvania who performed a double lung transplant on October 17, 2012. After the surgery she needed rehabilitation for six months. Her faith and the support of her family and friends gave her strength. She had a positive outlook, never gave up and fought every step of the way. She has now completed seven years post-transplant surgery, an impressive milestone. She just keeps going. She and her husband have been active community residents. Srinivasan served as an able president of our housing association for two years. Vijaya has helped organize both a music club and a ladies' club here. She also helped to organize ladies club activities such as yoga, and arts and crafts. Vijaya said "Life is not easy. It is similar to a river you travel with lots of winding turns and obstacles along the way. We are here to travel that river, learn along the way and enjoy what we can. Life's challenges grow our spirits and bring us closer to the divine." I felt that their life was a fine example of courage, faith, fortitude, adaptation, love and service to others. They have taught us how to face life's problems.

Of course, illness is not the only hardship. There are a few widows and widowers who are living alone and have had to adapt to losing the companionship of their spouses. Their feeling of loneliness is often lessened by the company and support of the residents. This is true for most residents, since our children are busy with their careers and raising their children. But since our association is a 55 plus active retirement community, residents are required to be independent and be able to drive especially to doctor's appointments and not be a hazard to other residents. Many times their healthy spouse looks after them if they are partially disabled. I have noticed that some residents with severe illnesses who could not look after themselves and do activities of daily living, have moved closer to their children in other states. There are a few people who have remarried after the death of a spouse and it is always comforting to see them adjusting and getting along well with their new spouses.

As for Meena and me, we have been thoroughly enjoying our retired life in Shantiniketan and blessed that we still have one another's love and companionship. We have been taking advantage of our relatively good health and mostly look forward to visiting our children and grandchildren. They do not live close by, so we try and see them at least every three months. Many times when we see each other, we choose to take vacations at beachside destinations. It especially makes us feel good when our children compliment us for being good parents and setting a good example for them. I hope they mean it! Meena and I are grateful to God for giving us nice daughters who have talented and caring husbands, who we consider our sons, as well as for our grandchildren Raya, Ayana, Sahana and Saavan. They are treasures and we love playing and talking with them.

We enjoy visiting Shefali and my granddaughters, Raya and Ayana, whenever possible in Chicago. It is fun attending their school events and graduation parties with all the youngsters around. Raya is 18 years old and has recently graduated from her high school and is a freshman at The Ohio State University. She is a proud Buckeye, just like her dad and me. In high school years she had a third-degree black belt in TaeKwonDo and was also a member of her school's diving and water polo teams. I was impressed with her courage to pick up these new competitive water sports in high school even though she had never played these sports before. Ayana is just 14 years old and a high school freshman. She has a second-degree black belt in TaeKwonDo. I am very careful in wrestling with these kids in case they give me a karate kick! Ayana is a talented dancer and it is very special for us to watch when she performs at some of our bigger gatherings.

My younger daughter, Shilpi, and her two children reside in Macon, Georgia, which is much closer to us. Sahana, who is 10 years old, and Saavan, who is 7 years old, follow their cousins' footsteps and take TaeKwonDo. Sahana is a creative and sensitive girl with an artist's mind. She enjoys creating art, playing the piano, and Bollywood and Indian classical dancing. She also has a soft spot for animals. Saavan has a sharp mind and loves anything having to do with wheels...bikes, cars, etc. He knew every major make and model of car and airplane by the age of three! We enjoy our grandchildren's innocence and are amazed at their playful energy. Our daughters and sons-in-laws are good parents, actively involved in their children's activities despite their busy professional careers. We are proud of our family. We have been truly blessed.

With Grandchildren in Mt. Dora, Florida

CHAPTER 24

GOLDEN YEARS

Food Drive for the Homeless in Orlando, Florida

Over the years I have read spiritual books or quotations from great people about the benefits of selfless service. A quote from Tagore says "I slept and dreamt that life was joy. I awoke and saw that life was service. I acted and behold, service was joy."

In December of 2016, I found out that there was a clinic nearby run by a charitable organization. It provides quality service to indigent patients who have no insurance and do not qualify for government aid. The physicians who volunteer there include general practitioners, internists and specialists in neurology, orthopedics and dermatology. I was interviewed by the clinic's pleasant and competent manager and I inquired whether they needed a psychiatrist a few hours a week. She agreed they could use my expertise. So, I worked there one day a week for nearly two years leaving me more than enough time for my retirement routines of exercising, playing cards and socializing. This arrangement also allowed me to take frequent vacations with my family.

The clinic had a sizable Hispanic patient population who did not speak English. Many of the voluntary ancillary and clerical staff were bilingual and worked with me as interpreters. The clinic had paper charts and I took my own time in taking a detailed history and treating the patient. This was a nice change and felt good to be able to work in this way. On a daily basis, many physicians who work in private practice or other medical settings, often feel the tension between shuttling patients through the clinic to achieve personal and institutional financial goals, versus taking the time they need with patients so that they might be fully seen, heard, and appropriately cared for. Many psychiatrists are also going through the same dilemma. The result is that ultimately the patient does not get excellent care and suffers. It also leads to physician burnout. I am a life fellow of the American Psychiatric Association and a member of the West Virginia Psychiatric Association for many years. Recently I have joined the Florida Psychiatric society. Through these organizations I have tried to be an advocate for psychiatry and our patients. The various players in the healthcare system, such as health insurance companies, managed care organizations, hospitals, pharmaceutical industries, attorneys, government agencies, and other medical organizations, like the American Medical Association and American Psychiatric Association, need to come together and ensure that physicians are able to provide more of their time and resources toward patient care rather than on bureaucratic computer and documentation work.

At the charitable clinic, besides medication management I also had the time to do brief psychotherapy and refer the patient to the clinic's counselor, if needed. The patients were grateful that somebody cared for them and took time to listen instead of looking at the computer and typing their progress notes. Many of these patients have felt neglected and faced a lot of hardships and stressors which made them depressed and anxious. I found out that doing this type of voluntary service was joyful and gratifying to me. I also had the feeling that I was giving back in a very small way to the society and country which has given me so much. I wish I could go back to India and provide free psychiatric services to the poor in the slums. But after living in the US for so many years, I worry that with my health and age, I would find it difficult to adjust.

Now since I have retired and reached the sunset of my life, I am looking back over the years to see what I have achieved and the people who have influenced my life. I have lived in three countries (India, Great Britain and the US) and have been influenced by these three very diverse cultures. While many residents in Shantiniketan are interested in watching Indian movies, serials and cricket, I am also interested in old Hollywood movies, PBS, British comedy shows and sports, especially golf and football. I have tried to take the best from these cultures.

Facing my many challenges and my shortcomings was not easy. But I was determined to achieve self-growth by learning and putting into practice the ideas and therapies proposed by leading mental health professionals such as Erik Erikson, Aaron Beck, Abraham Maslow, and psychopharmacologists like Drs. Stephen Stahl, Henry Nasrallah, Rakesh Jain and Alan Gelenburg. These practices helped me to be a better person. After initial years of learning and difficult life experiences, I was able to perform my work with confidence. As a result, along the way, I was complimented by my superiors and fellow employees about my knowledge of psychiatry and my work ethic.

I was also a fervent reader of spiritual books of various religions. I have read the Bible, the Hindu's Bhagavad Gita, Quran, the Buddhist Dhammapada, and Jain Agams. I have read commentaries on the Gita by several authors including Eknath Easwaran. I have been influenced by the Indian spiritual sects of Brahma Kumaris, Dada Bhagwan, Hindu, Buddhist and Jain philosophies and have read several books on these subjects. In addition, I have listened to many lectures by spiritual leaders. It was important to me that I also exposed my children to many of these religions and philosophies so that they may benefit from the different teachings, while also recognizing the commonalities within them all.

Mahatma Gandhi wisely said, 'Religions are different roads converging to the same point. What does it matter that we take different roads as long as we reach the same goal?" Instead of becoming confused by these spiritual paths, I was able to pick the good in each and try to put it in practice in my everyday life. I have tried to follow these divine qualities with limited success. It is a constant practice. I admire Christians for following the preaching of Jesus Christ, Hindus for following the teachings of Krishna and Shiva, Muslims for following the teachings of Muhammad and Allah and Jews for obeying Yahweh's teachings. I am impressed by Christianity's emphasis on love, hope and optimism and Hindus advice regarding overcoming anger, pride, greed and excessive desires. I liked the Buddha and Mahavir's paths of non-violence and compassion. These paths lead one to everlasting happiness. I have gained new spiritual insights from my good friends in Shantiniketan and have enjoyed working on food drives for the homeless in Orlando through the Jain Temple. I enjoy friendships of people of every religion. I am of the belief that people of all faiths and countries can get along with each other and avoid wars if they try hard and are open minded because there is good in every faith. I am a great admirer of preachers like Norman Vincent Peale, Robert Schuller, Billy Graham and Joel Osteen. I have read the "Power of Positive Thinking" by Peale a few times. I have also gained a lot of perspective from reading books by Deepak Chopra, Chitrabhanu, Deepakbhai Desai, and B.K. Shivani. My tendency to think negatively and pessimistically has been helped by reading books by these authors.

I have experienced mild episodes of anxiety and depression in my life, but they have not interfered with my work. I feel I may have inherited some of these traits from my mother who was an anxious person and had bouts of depression. My unhappy childhood experiences may have contributed to my having problems with relationships and anger during my youth. But I have tried to face these challenges in my life and improve myself. Reading spiritual and psychology books, as well as talking with friends has helped me to face these challenges. Presently, there is much anxiety surrounding the recent wave of coronavirus that is sweeping through nation. Because of my tendency to think of the worst case scenarios and the impact that this virus has on people my age, my faith and reading these kinds of books, help me face this pandemic with courage and optimism.

I was reflecting on my life based on the humanist psychologist, Abraham Maslow's, Hierarchy of Needs and by doing so, was able to view my life in a lens of gratefulness. I had read about him during my residency years. He talks about a pyramid of needs that people are motivated to fulfill so that they may move from one level to the next;

progressing from fulfilling physiological needs, to psychological and social needs, and ultimately toward self-actualization and transendence.

In my case, according to Maslow's theory, my safety and security needs were fulfilled when I obtained a steady job in peaceful West Virginia. I am also fortunate to be living in the best country in the world. I met my social belonging needs with a loving family and caring friends. I must thank my wife for her continued support and love through good and bad times. She is a great human being and a homemaker. She is popular in Shantiniketan because of her cheerful nature, positive attitude and readiness to help others. My self-esteem needs are satisfied because I feel respected as a psychiatrist, family man, a friend, and more recently for being elected to the board of the Shantiniketan Housing Association and being on the Health Committee. I am still working toward fulfilling the hierarchical phase of self-actualization. I have not accomplished everything I want yet, but I am satisfied and content with what I have achieved. I am still trying to achieve the last of Maslow's need, self-transcendence. This involves altruism and spirituality. My altruistic needs are partially satisfied by helping my patients, volunteering my services and helping others including the Shantiniketan residents.

I am appreciative of where I have reached in my life. I could not have reached here without constant perseverance, loving and supportive relationships, and by the grace of God. By reading spiritual books I have achieved some peace and tranquility in my life. When I do morning prayers and meditation, God bestows on me a feeling of divine bliss and peace. I try not to think about the future. I have come a long way and it has not been easy. As Tagore said, "When I stand before thee at the day's end, thou shall see my scars and know that I had my wounds and also my healing." I feel that I have now achieved peace and happiness in the evening of my life.

Vacationing with Shefali, Pranav, Shilpi, Arpan and
Grandchildren in Amelia Island, Florida

GIVE ME STRENGTH

This is my prayer to thee, my Lord — strike, strike at the root of penury in my heart.

Give me the strength lightly to bear my joys and sorrows.

Give me the strength to make my love fruitful in service.

Give me the strength never to disown the poor or bend my knees before insolent might.

Give me the strength to raise my mind high above daily trifles.

And give me the strength to surrender my strength to thy will with love.

—Rabindranath Tagore
In *Gitanjali*